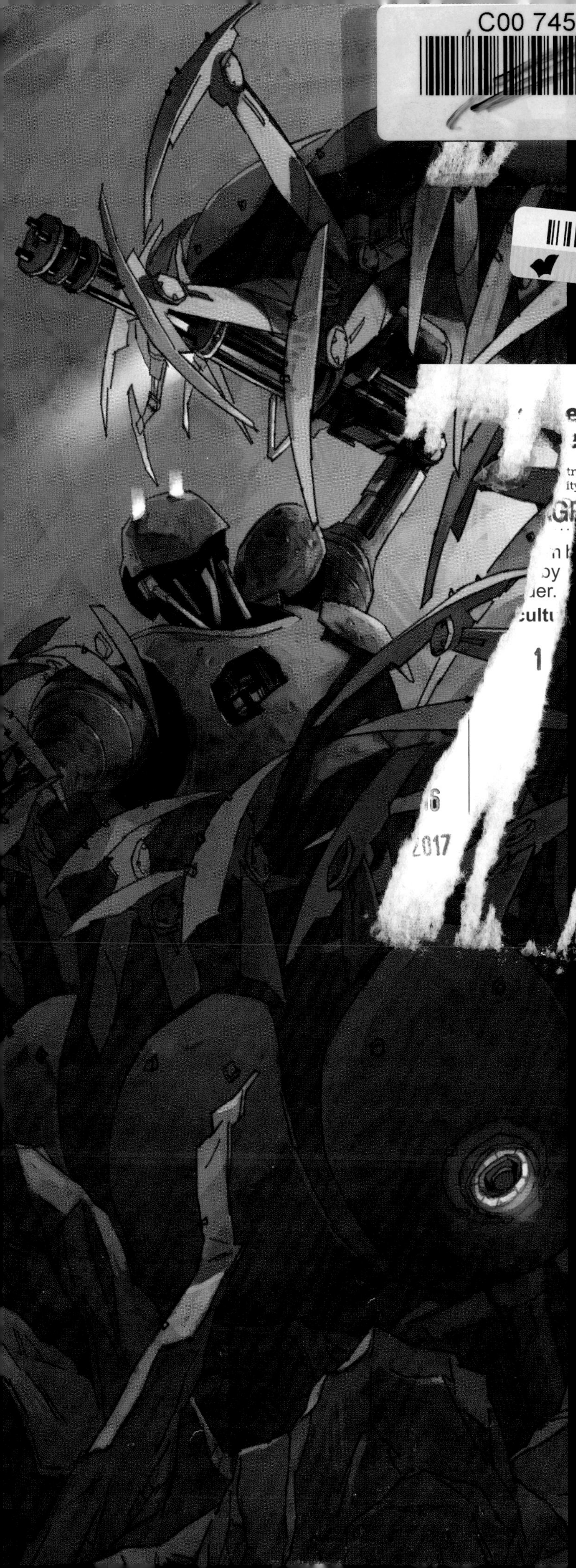

SAM 2

MARAZANO
SCRIPT
SHANG
ARTWORK AND COLOURS

ROBOT HUNTERS

Original title: Chasseurs de robot

Original edition: © Dargaud Paris 2013
by Marazano & Shang
www.dargaud.com
All rights reserved

English translation: © 2015 Cinebook Ltd

Translator: Jerome Saincantin
Lettering and text layout: Design Amorandi
Printed in Spain by EGEDSA

This edition first published in Great Britain in 2015 by
Cinebook Ltd
56 Beech Avenue
Canterbury, Kent
CT4 7TA
www.cinebook.com

A CIP catalogue record for this book
is available from the British Library

ISBN 978-1-84918-246-1

9th CINEBOOK
The 9th Art Publisher

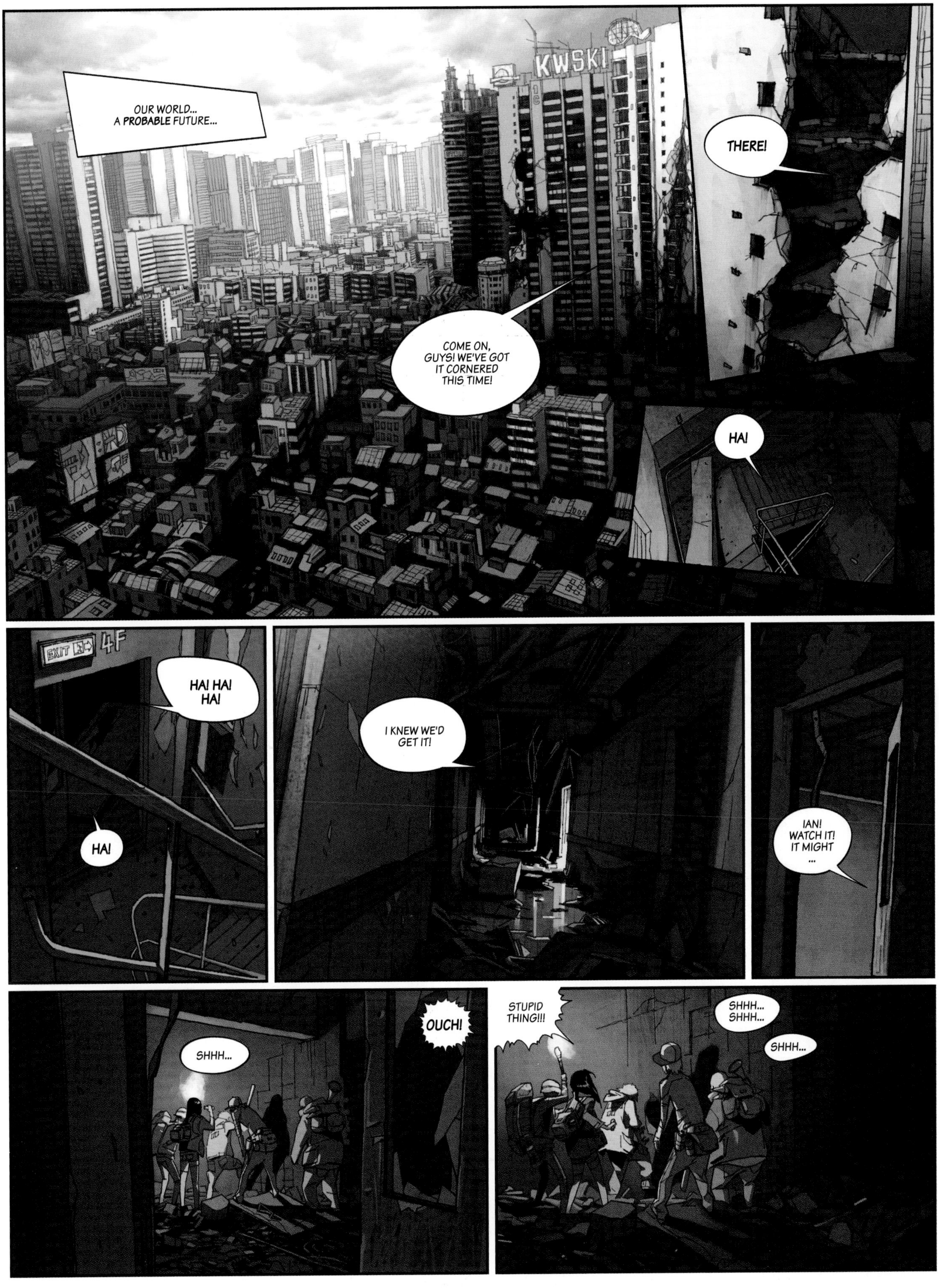
OUR WORLD...
A PROBABLE FUTURE...
KWSKI
COME ON, GUYS! WE'VE GOT IT CORNERED THIS TIME!
THERE!
HA!
EXIT 4F
HA! HA! HA!
HA!
I KNEW WE'D GET IT!
IAN! WATCH IT! IT MIGHT ...
SHHH...
OUCH!
STUPID THING!!!
SHHH... SHHH...
SHHH...

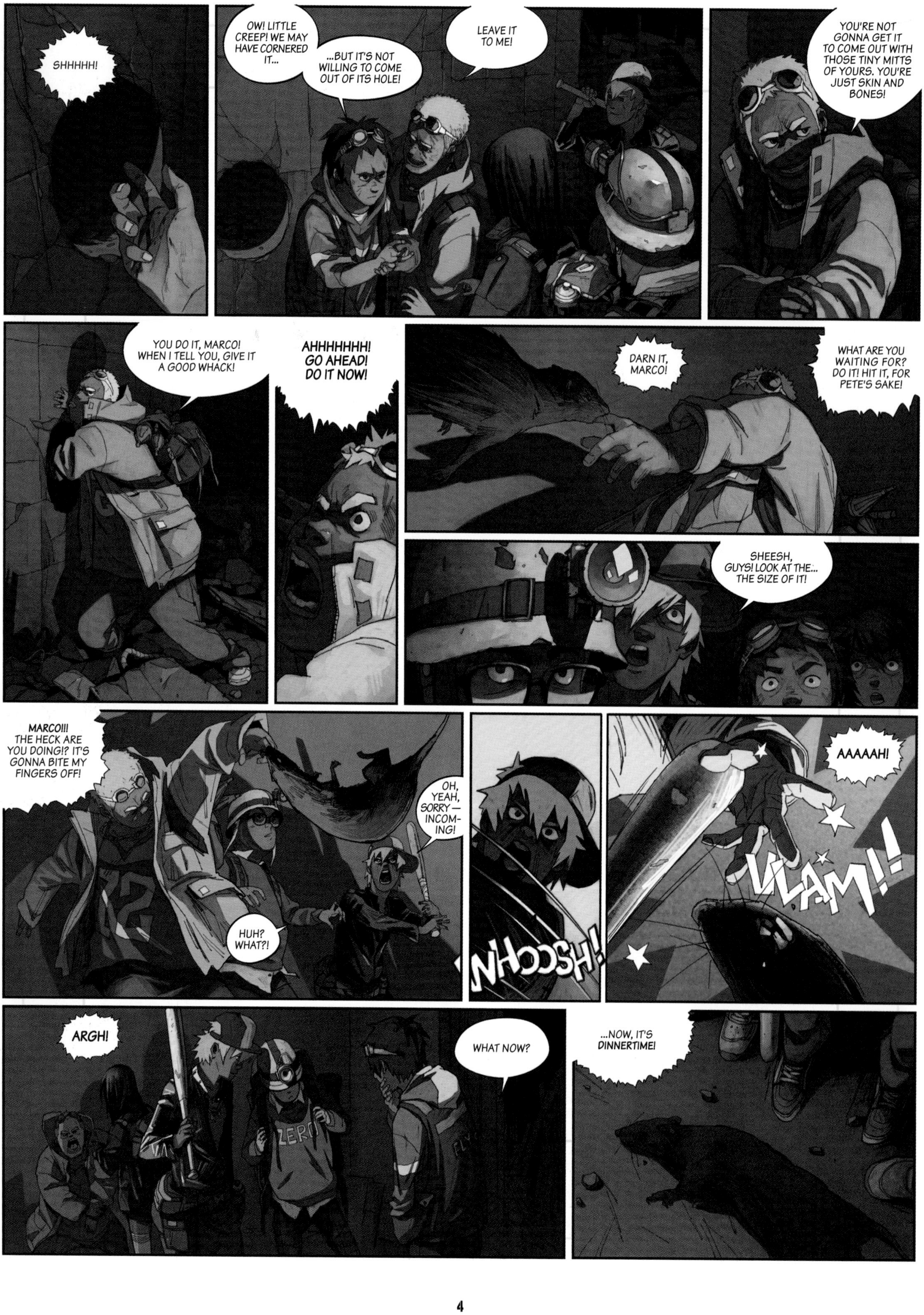
SHHHHH!
OW! LITTLE CREEP! WE MAY HAVE CORNERED IT...
...BUT IT'S NOT WILLING TO COME OUT OF ITS HOLE!
LEAVE IT TO ME!
YOU'RE NOT GONNA GET IT TO COME OUT WITH THOSE TINY MITTS OF YOURS. YOU'RE JUST SKIN AND BONES!
YOU DO IT, MARCO! WHEN I TELL YOU, GIVE IT A GOOD WHACK!
AHHHHHHH! GO AHEAD! DO IT NOW!
DARN IT, MARCO!
WHAT ARE YOU WAITING FOR? DO IT! HIT IT, FOR PETE'S SAKE!
SHEESH, GUYS! LOOK AT THE... THE SIZE OF IT!
MARCO!!! THE HECK ARE YOU DOING!? IT'S GONNA BITE MY FINGERS OFF!
OH, YEAH, SORRY— INCOM-ING!
HUH? WHAT?!
WHOOSH!
AAAAAH!
VLAM!!
ARGH!
WHAT NOW?
...NOW, IT'S DINNERTIME!

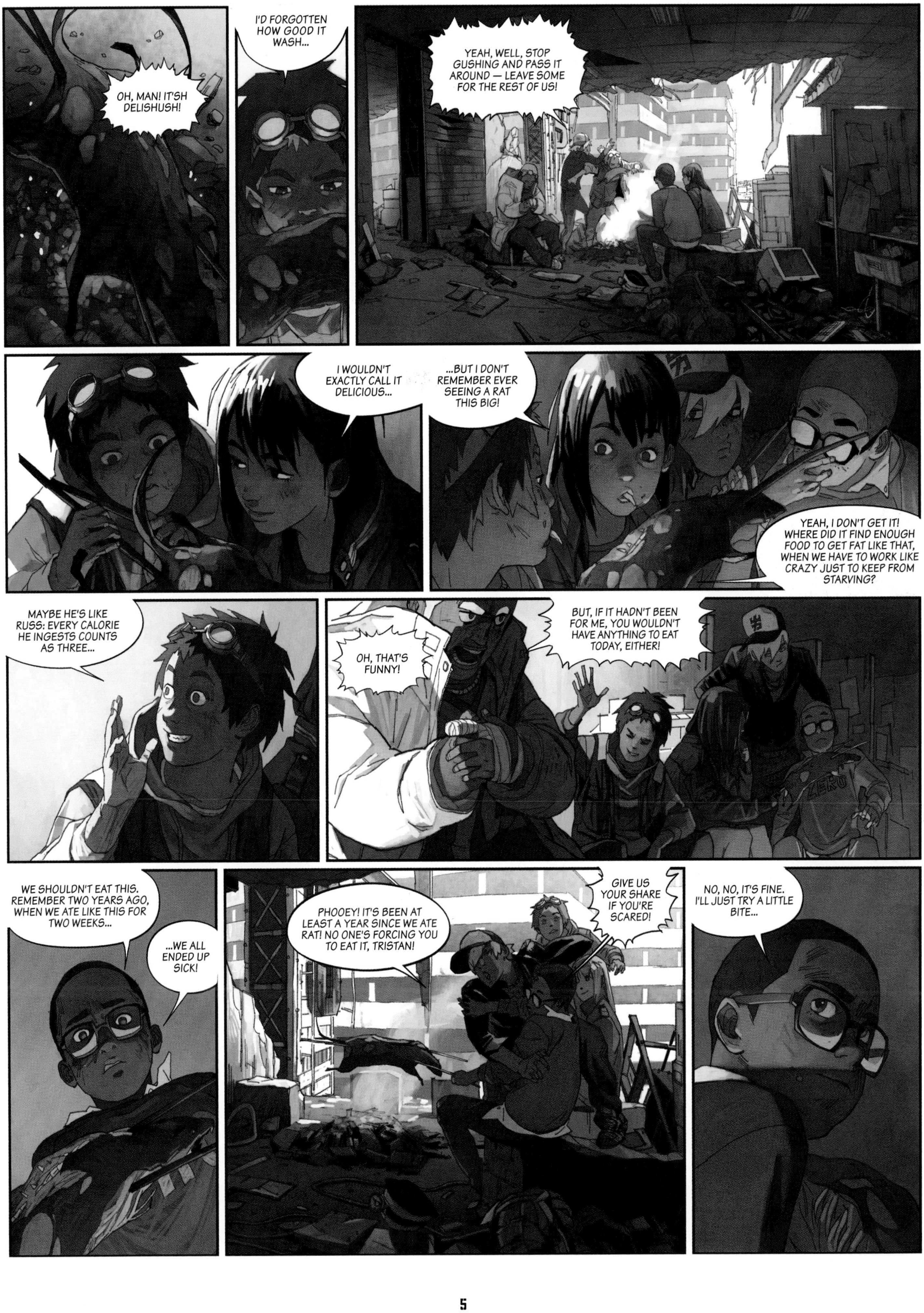
OH, MAN! IT'SH DELISHUSH!
I'D FORGOTTEN HOW GOOD IT WASH...
YEAH, WELL, STOP GUSHING AND PASS IT AROUND — LEAVE SOME FOR THE REST OF US!
I WOULDN'T EXACTLY CALL IT DELICIOUS...
...BUT I DON'T REMEMBER EVER SEEING A RAT THIS BIG!
YEAH, I DON'T GET IT! WHERE DID IT FIND ENOUGH FOOD TO GET FAT LIKE THAT, WHEN WE HAVE TO WORK LIKE CRAZY JUST TO KEEP FROM STARVING?
MAYBE HE'S LIKE RUSS: EVERY CALORIE HE INGESTS COUNTS AS THREE...
OH, THAT'S FUNNY!
BUT, IF IT HADN'T BEEN FOR ME, YOU WOULDN'T HAVE ANYTHING TO EAT TODAY, EITHER!
WE SHOULDN'T EAT THIS. REMEMBER TWO YEARS AGO, WHEN WE ATE LIKE THIS FOR TWO WEEKS...
...WE ALL ENDED UP SICK!
PHOOEY! IT'S BEEN AT LEAST A YEAR SINCE WE ATE RAT! NO ONE'S FORCING YOU TO EAT IT, TRISTAN!
GIVE US YOUR SHARE IF YOU'RE SCARED!
NO, NO, IT'S FINE. I'LL JUST TRY A LITTLE BITE...

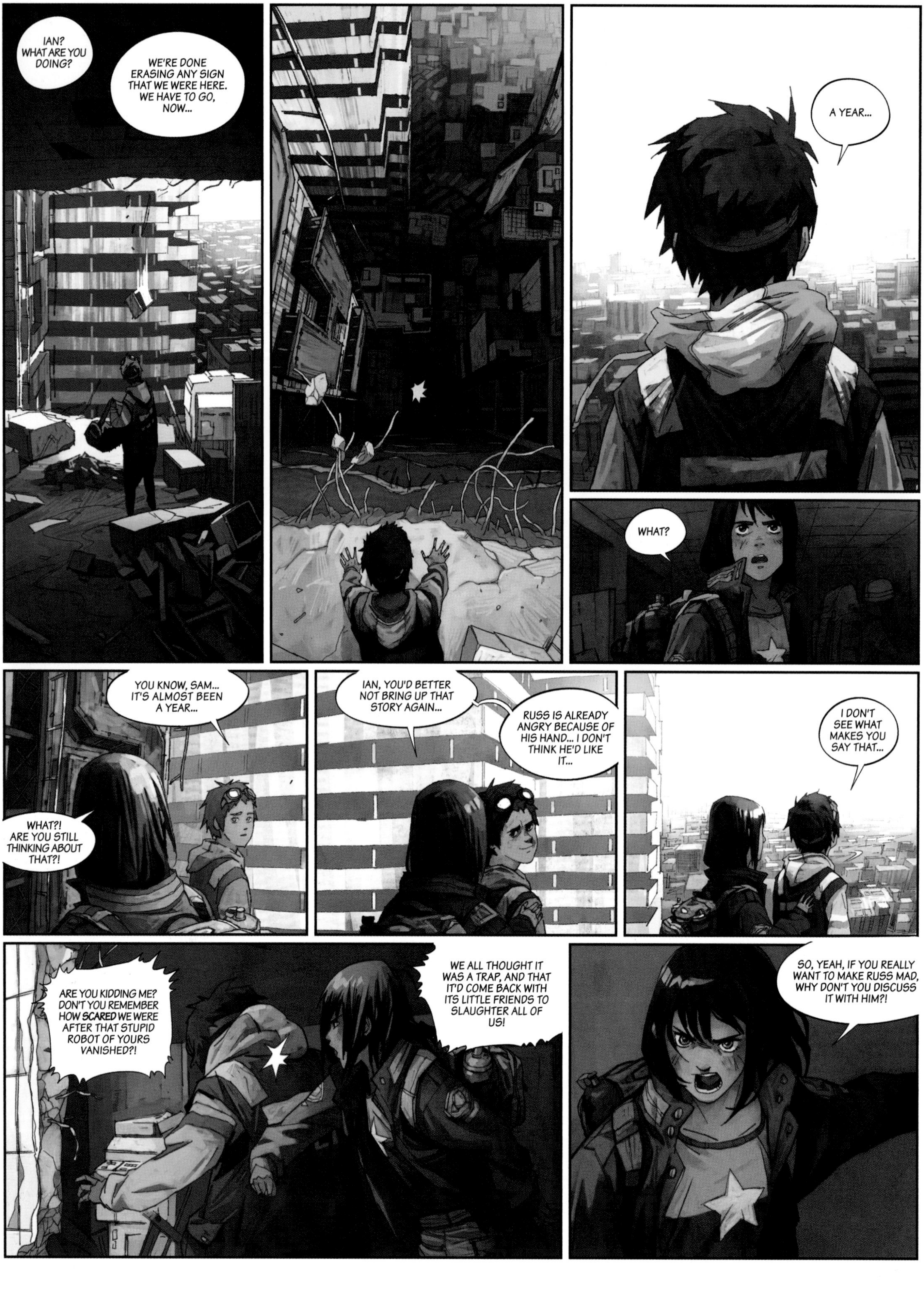
IAN? WHAT ARE YOU DOING?
WE'RE DONE ERASING ANY SIGN THAT WE WERE HERE. WE HAVE TO GO, NOW...
A YEAR...
WHAT?
YOU KNOW, SAM... IT'S ALMOST BEEN A YEAR...
WHAT?! ARE YOU STILL THINKING ABOUT THAT?!
IAN, YOU'D BETTER NOT BRING UP THAT STORY AGAIN...
RUSS IS ALREADY ANGRY BECAUSE OF HIS HAND... I DON'T THINK HE'D LIKE IT...
I DON'T SEE WHAT MAKES YOU SAY THAT...
ARE YOU KIDDING ME? DON'T YOU REMEMBER HOW SCARED WE WERE AFTER THAT STUPID ROBOT OF YOURS VANISHED?!
WE ALL THOUGHT IT WAS A TRAP, AND THAT IT'D COME BACK WITH ITS LITTLE FRIENDS TO SLAUGHTER ALL OF US!
SO, YEAH, IF YOU REALLY WANT TO MAKE RUSS MAD, WHY DON'T YOU DISCUSS IT WITH HIM?!

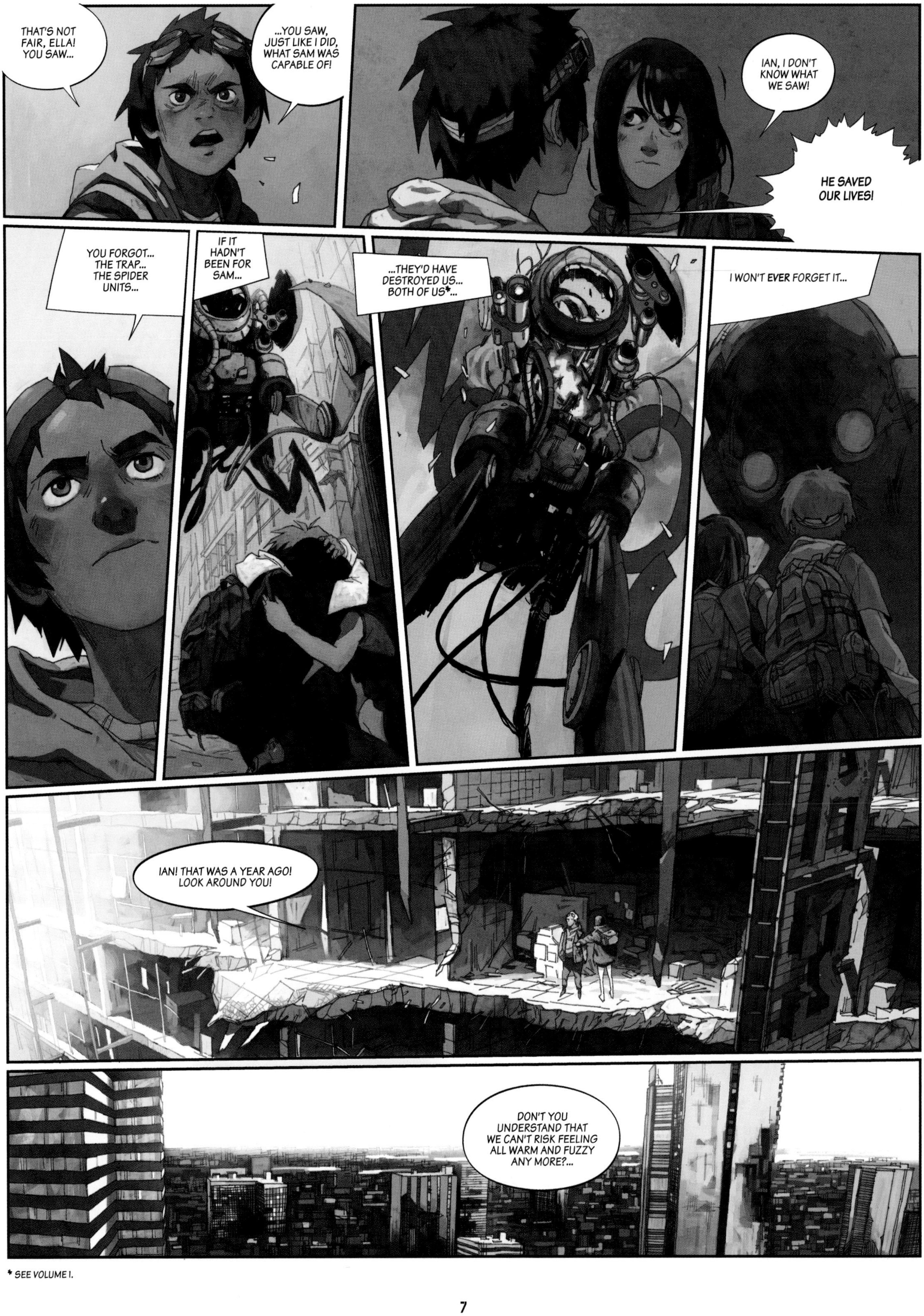
THAT'S NOT FAIR, ELLA! YOU SAW...
...YOU SAW, JUST LIKE I DID, WHAT SAM WAS CAPABLE OF!
IAN, I DON'T KNOW WHAT WE SAW!
HE SAVED OUR LIVES!
YOU FORGOT... THE TRAP... THE SPIDER UNITS...
IF IT HADN'T BEEN FOR SAM...
...THEY'D HAVE DESTROYED US... BOTH OF US*...
I WON'T EVER FORGET IT...
IAN! THAT WAS A YEAR AGO! LOOK AROUND YOU!
DON'T YOU UNDERSTAND THAT WE CAN'T RISK FEELING ALL WARM AND FUZZY ANY MORE?...

* SEE VOLUME 1.

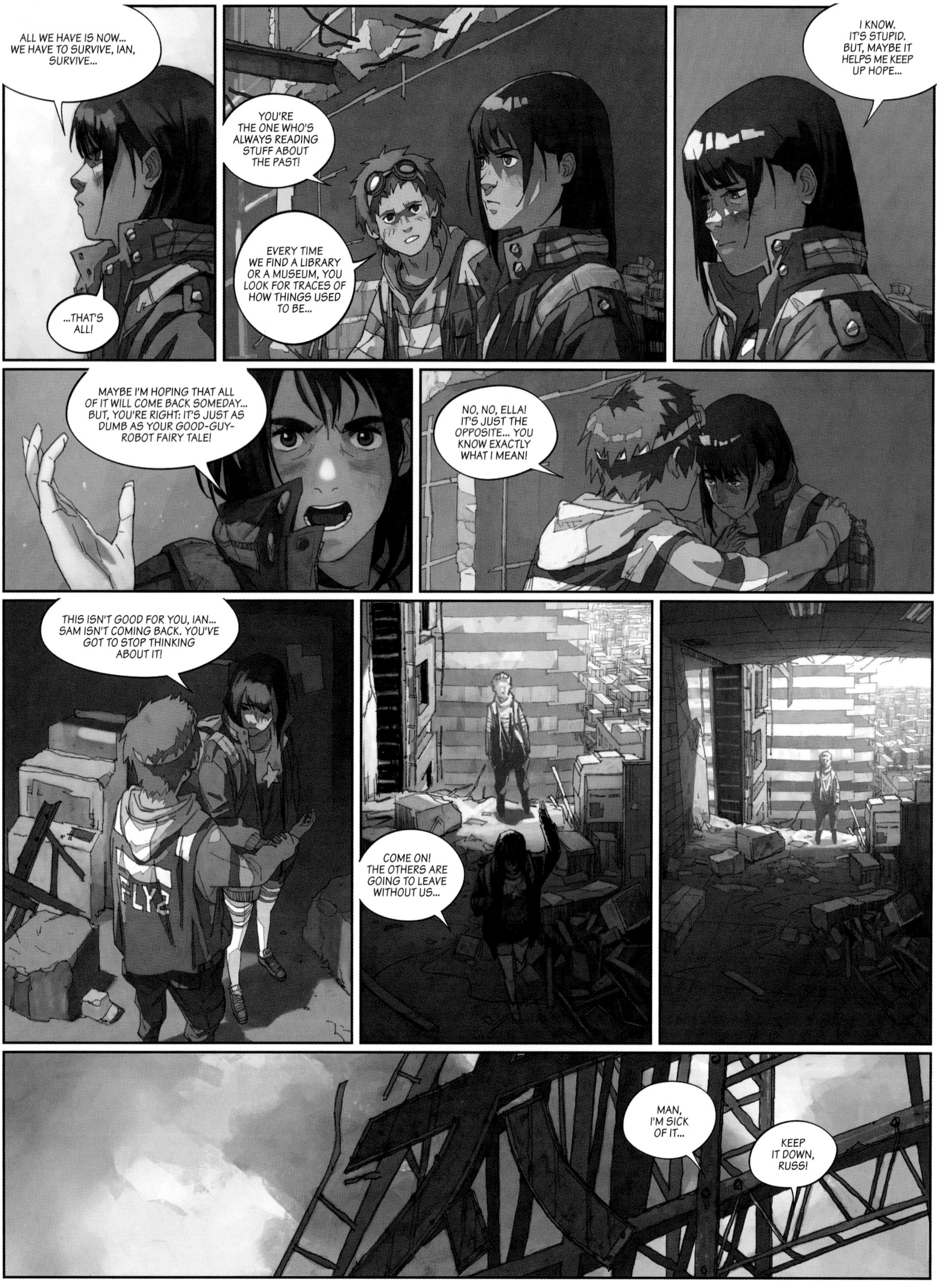
ALL WE HAVE IS NOW... WE HAVE TO SURVIVE, IAN, SURVIVE...
...THAT'S ALL!
YOU'RE THE ONE WHO'S ALWAYS READING STUFF ABOUT THE PAST!
EVERY TIME WE FIND A LIBRARY OR A MUSEUM, YOU LOOK FOR TRACES OF HOW THINGS USED TO BE...
I KNOW. IT'S STUPID. BUT, MAYBE IT HELPS ME KEEP UP HOPE...
MAYBE I'M HOPING THAT ALL OF IT WILL COME BACK SOMEDAY... BUT, YOU'RE RIGHT: IT'S JUST AS DUMB AS YOUR GOOD-GUY-ROBOT FAIRY TALE!
NO, NO, ELLA! IT'S JUST THE OPPOSITE... YOU KNOW EXACTLY WHAT I MEAN!
THIS ISN'T GOOD FOR YOU, IAN... SAM ISN'T COMING BACK. YOU'VE GOT TO STOP THINKING ABOUT IT!
FLY2
COME ON! THE OTHERS ARE GOING TO LEAVE WITHOUT US...
MAN, I'M SICK OF IT...
KEEP IT DOWN, RUSS!

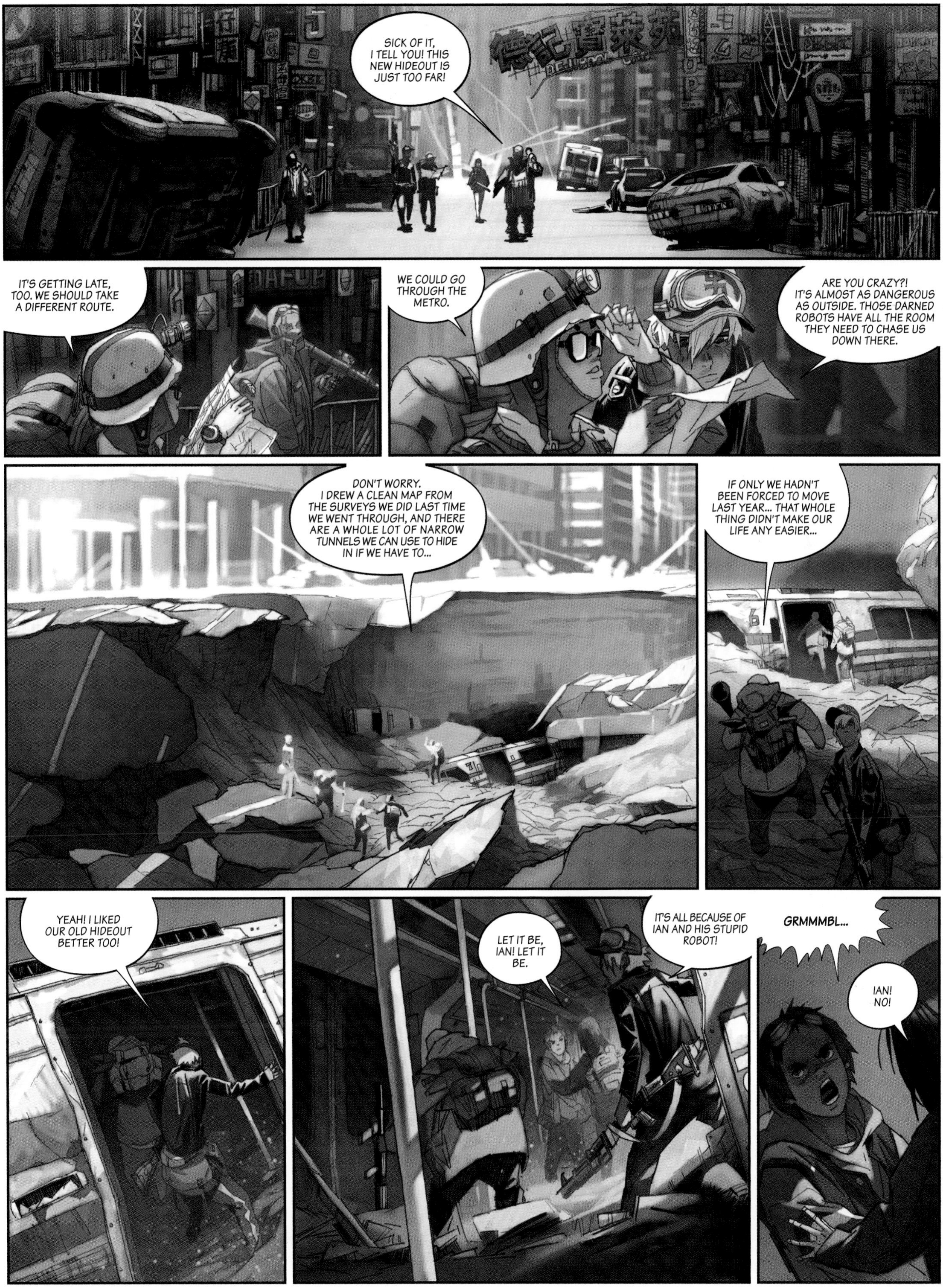
SICK OF IT, I TELL YOU! THIS NEW HIDEOUT IS JUST TOO FAR!
IT'S GETTING LATE, TOO. WE SHOULD TAKE A DIFFERENT ROUTE.
WE COULD GO THROUGH THE METRO.
ARE YOU CRAZY?! IT'S ALMOST AS DANGEROUS AS OUTSIDE. THOSE DARNED ROBOTS HAVE ALL THE ROOM THEY NEED TO CHASE US DOWN THERE.
DON'T WORRY. I DREW A CLEAN MAP FROM THE SURVEYS WE DID LAST TIME WE WENT THROUGH, AND THERE ARE A WHOLE LOT OF NARROW TUNNELS WE CAN USE TO HIDE IN IF WE HAVE TO...
IF ONLY WE HADN'T BEEN FORCED TO MOVE LAST YEAR... THAT WHOLE THING DIDN'T MAKE OUR LIFE ANY EASIER...
YEAH! I LIKED OUR OLD HIDEOUT BETTER TOO!
LET IT BE, IAN! LET IT BE.
IT'S ALL BECAUSE OF IAN AND HIS STUPID ROBOT!
GRMMMBL...
IAN! NO!

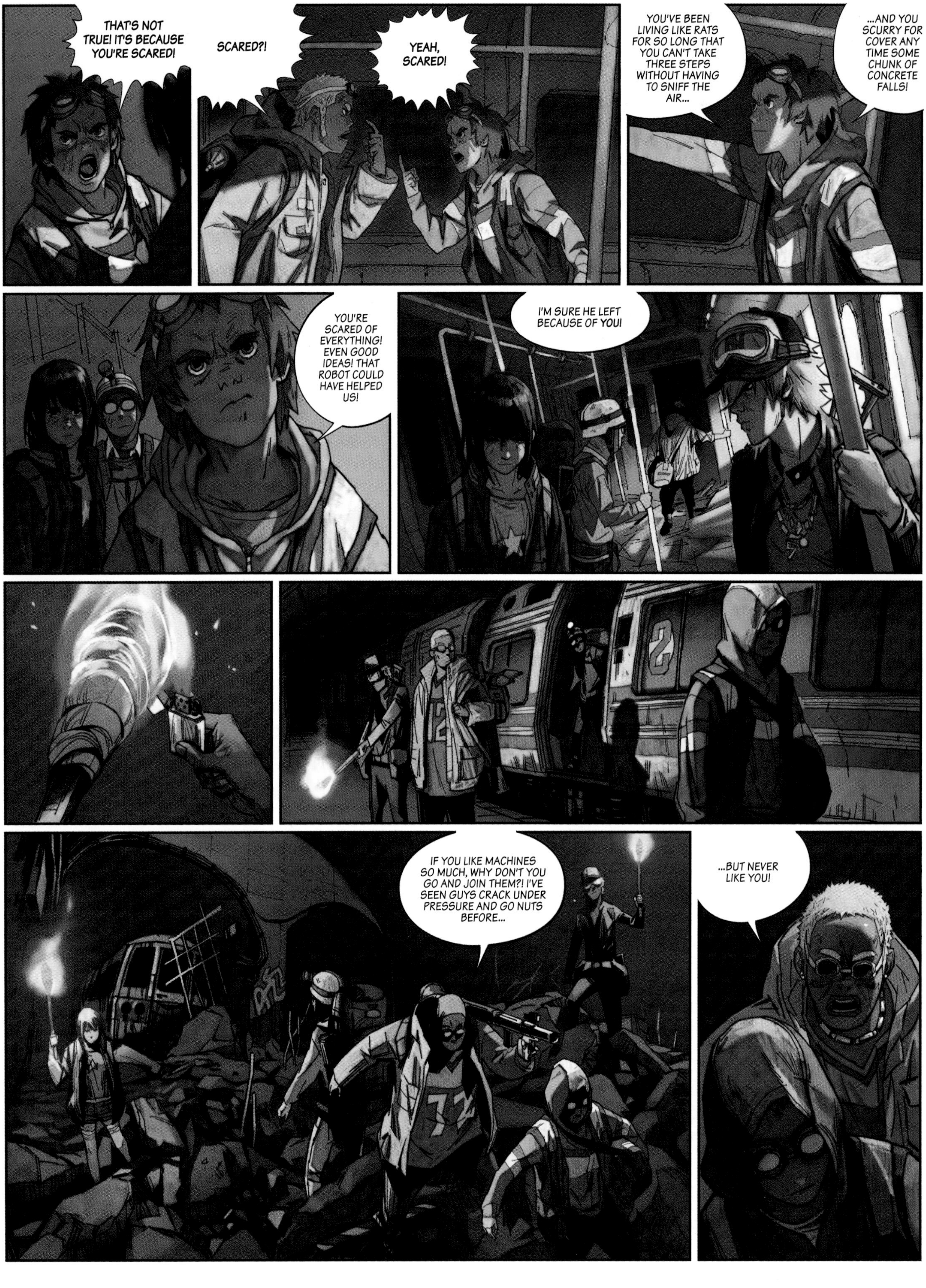
THAT'S NOT TRUE! IT'S BECAUSE YOU'RE SCARED!
SCARED?!
YEAH, SCARED!
YOU'VE BEEN LIVING LIKE RATS FOR SO LONG THAT YOU CAN'T TAKE THREE STEPS WITHOUT HAVING TO SNIFF THE AIR...
...AND YOU SCURRY FOR COVER ANY TIME SOME CHUNK OF CONCRETE FALLS!
YOU'RE SCARED OF EVERYTHING! EVEN GOOD IDEAS! THAT ROBOT COULD HAVE HELPED US!
I'M SURE HE LEFT BECAUSE OF YOU!
IF YOU LIKE MACHINES SO MUCH, WHY DON'T YOU GO AND JOIN THEM?! I'VE SEEN GUYS CRACK UNDER PRESSURE AND GO NUTS BEFORE...
...BUT NEVER LIKE YOU!

HERE'S A SCOOP FOR YOU: YEAH, WE DO LIVE LIKE RATS! AND, YEAH, WE SNIFF THE AIR EVERYWHERE. THAT'S BECAUSE WE DON'T WANT TO END UP CORNERED AND SKEWERED!

THAT'S NOT FEAR: THAT'S ADAPTATION! IT'S CALLED SURVIVAL INSTINCT!

BRROOOO—

AND IF YOU WANT TO SURVIVE, IAN, YOU'RE GONNA HAVE TO ADAPT!

DID YOU HEAR THAT?!

A TRAIN? THEY HAVEN'T RUN FOR...

OH, NO, NO...

BRRRRROOOMMM BRRR

CRAP! WE HAVE TO MOVE!

BRRROOMM BRRR

HURRY UP! RUN!

THIS WAY! FOLLOW ME! I KNOW A PASSAGE!

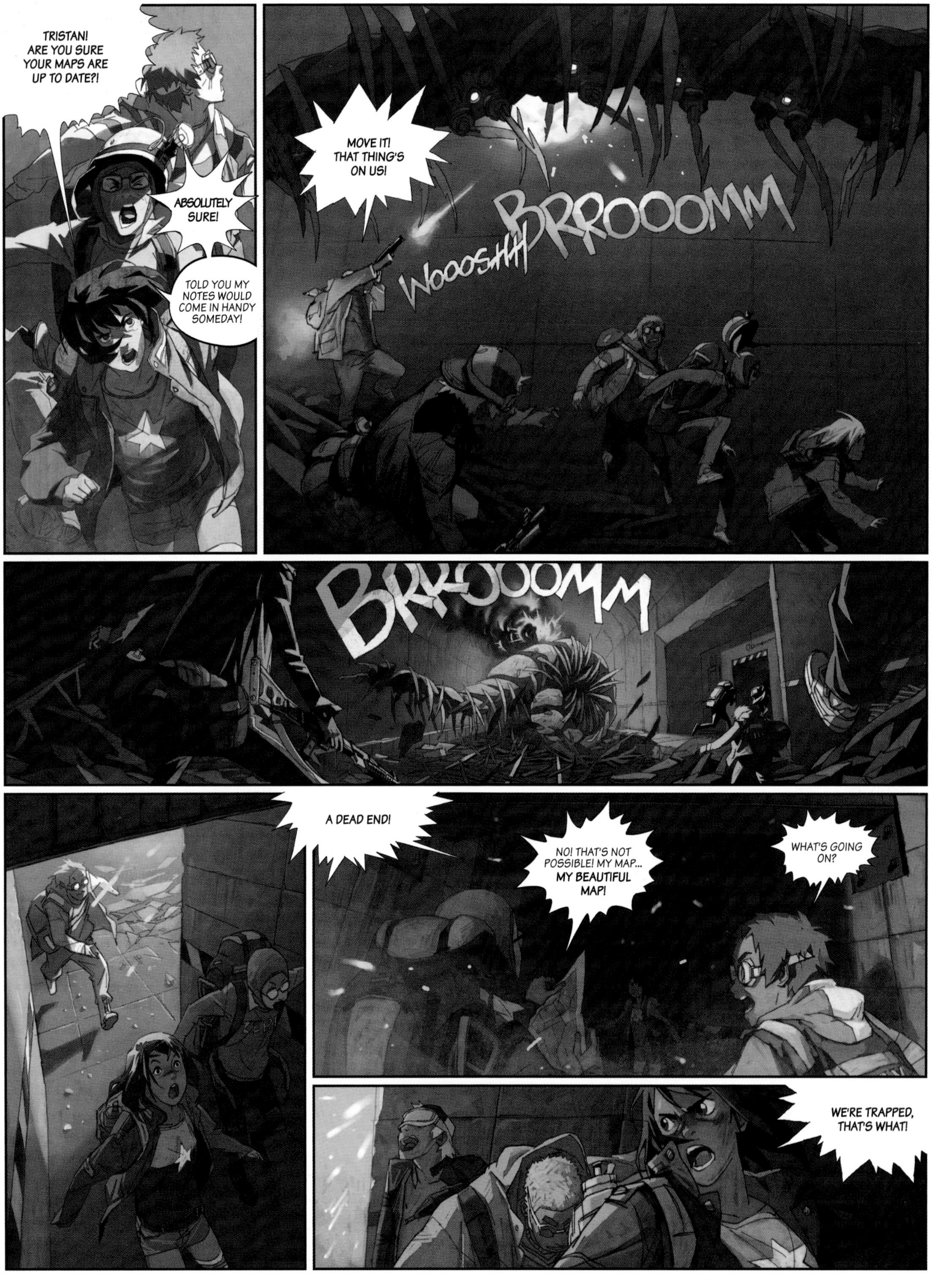

TRISTAN! ARE YOU SURE YOUR MAPS ARE UP TO DATE?!
ABSOLUTELY SURE!
TOLD YOU MY NOTES WOULD COME IN HANDY SOMEDAY!
MOVE IT! THAT THING'S ON US!
WOOOSHHH
BRROOOMM
BRROOOMM
A DEAD END!
NO! THAT'S NOT POSSIBLE! MY MAP... MY BEAUTIFUL MAP!
WHAT'S GOING ON?
WE'RE TRAPPED, THAT'S WHAT!

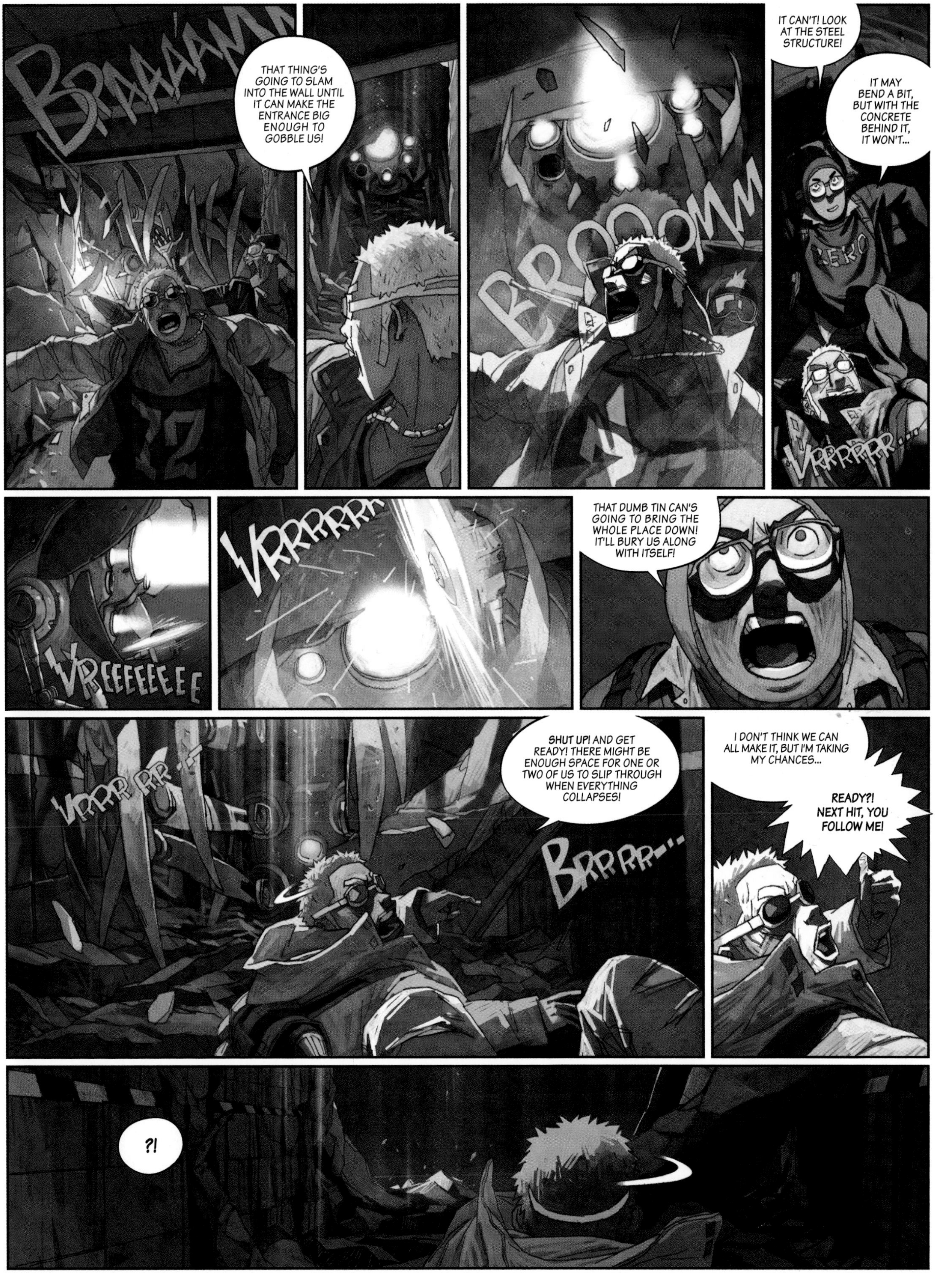
BRAAAAM
THAT THING'S GOING TO SLAM INTO THE WALL UNTIL IT CAN MAKE THE ENTRANCE BIG ENOUGH TO GOBBLE US!
BROOOMM
IT CAN'T! LOOK AT THE STEEL STRUCTURE!
IT MAY BEND A BIT, BUT WITH THE CONCRETE BEHIND IT, IT WON'T...
VRRRRRR...
VREEEEEEEE
VRRRRRR
THAT DUMB TIN CAN'S GOING TO BRING THE WHOLE PLACE DOWN! IT'LL BURY US ALONG WITH ITSELF!
VRRR RR
SHUT UP! AND GET READY! THERE MIGHT BE ENOUGH SPACE FOR ONE OR TWO OF US TO SLIP THROUGH WHEN EVERYTHING COLLAPSES!
BRRRR...
I DON'T THINK WE CAN ALL MAKE IT, BUT I'M TAKING MY CHANCES...
READY?! NEXT HIT, YOU FOLLOW ME!
?!

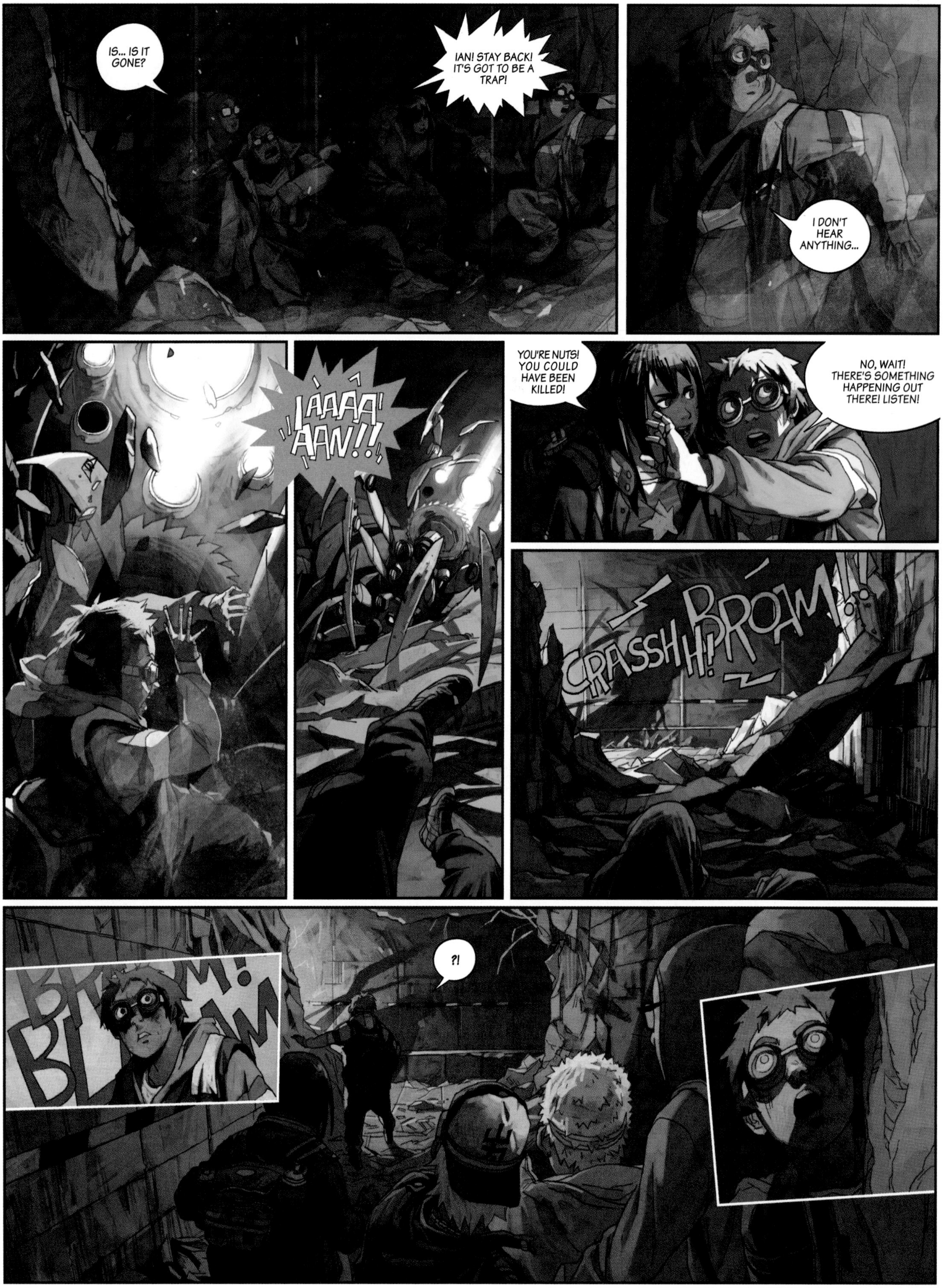
IS... IS IT GONE?
IAN! STAY BACK! IT'S GOT TO BE A TRAP!
I DON'T HEAR ANYTHING...
IAAAAAAN!!
YOU'RE NUTS! YOU COULD HAVE BEEN KILLED!
NO, WAIT! THERE'S SOMETHING HAPPENING OUT THERE! LISTEN!
CRASSHH! BROAM!!
?!
BROOM! BLAM

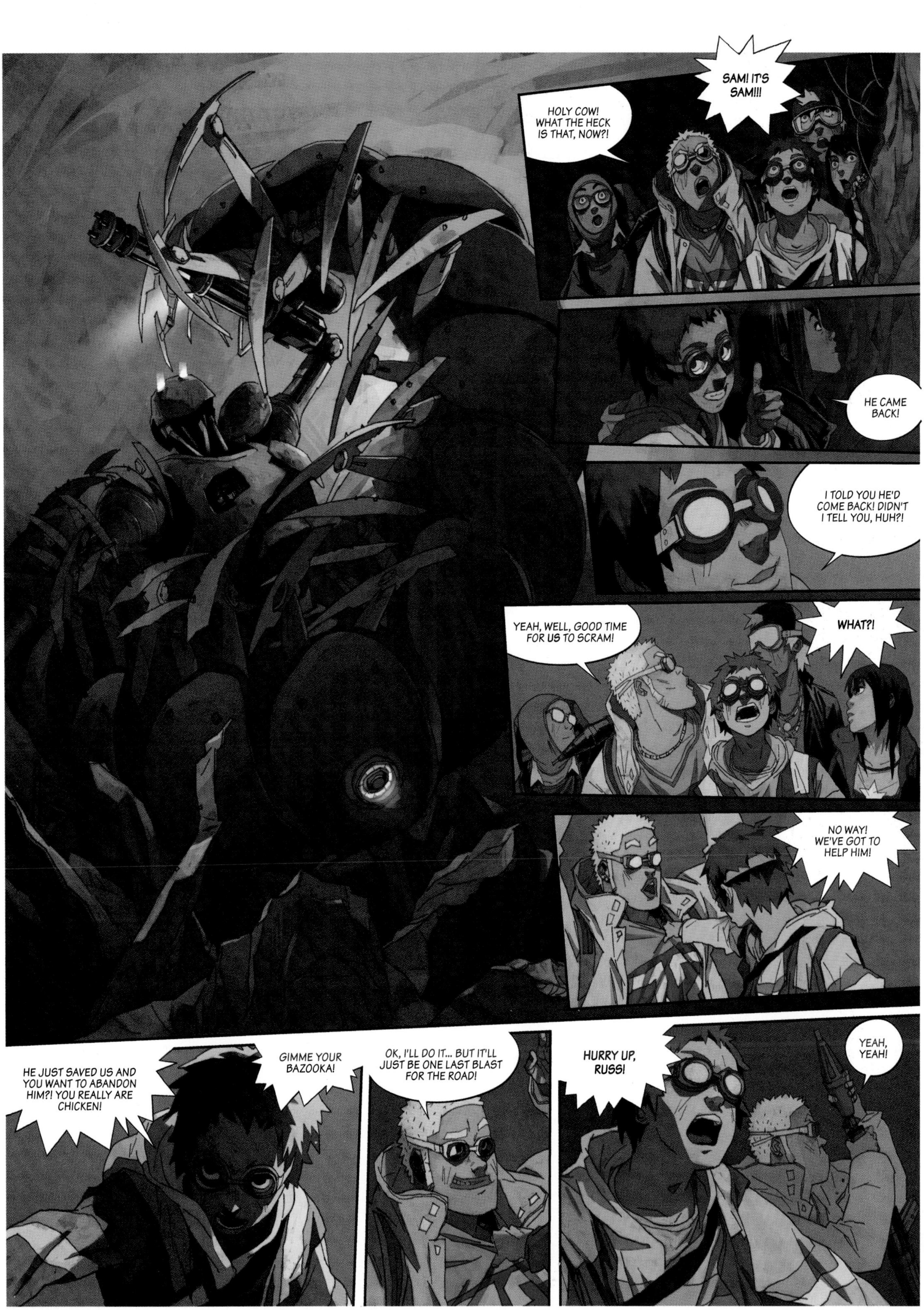

HOLY COW! WHAT THE HECK IS THAT, NOW?!
SAM! IT'S SAM!!!
HE CAME BACK!
I TOLD YOU HE'D COME BACK! DIDN'T I TELL YOU, HUH?!
YEAH, WELL, GOOD TIME FOR US TO SCRAM!
WHAT?!
NO WAY! WE'VE GOT TO HELP HIM!
HE JUST SAVED US AND YOU WANT TO ABANDON HIM?! YOU REALLY ARE CHICKEN!
GIMME YOUR BAZOOKA!
OK, I'LL DO IT... BUT IT'LL JUST BE ONE LAST BLAST FOR THE ROAD!
HURRY UP, RUSS!
YEAH, YEAH!

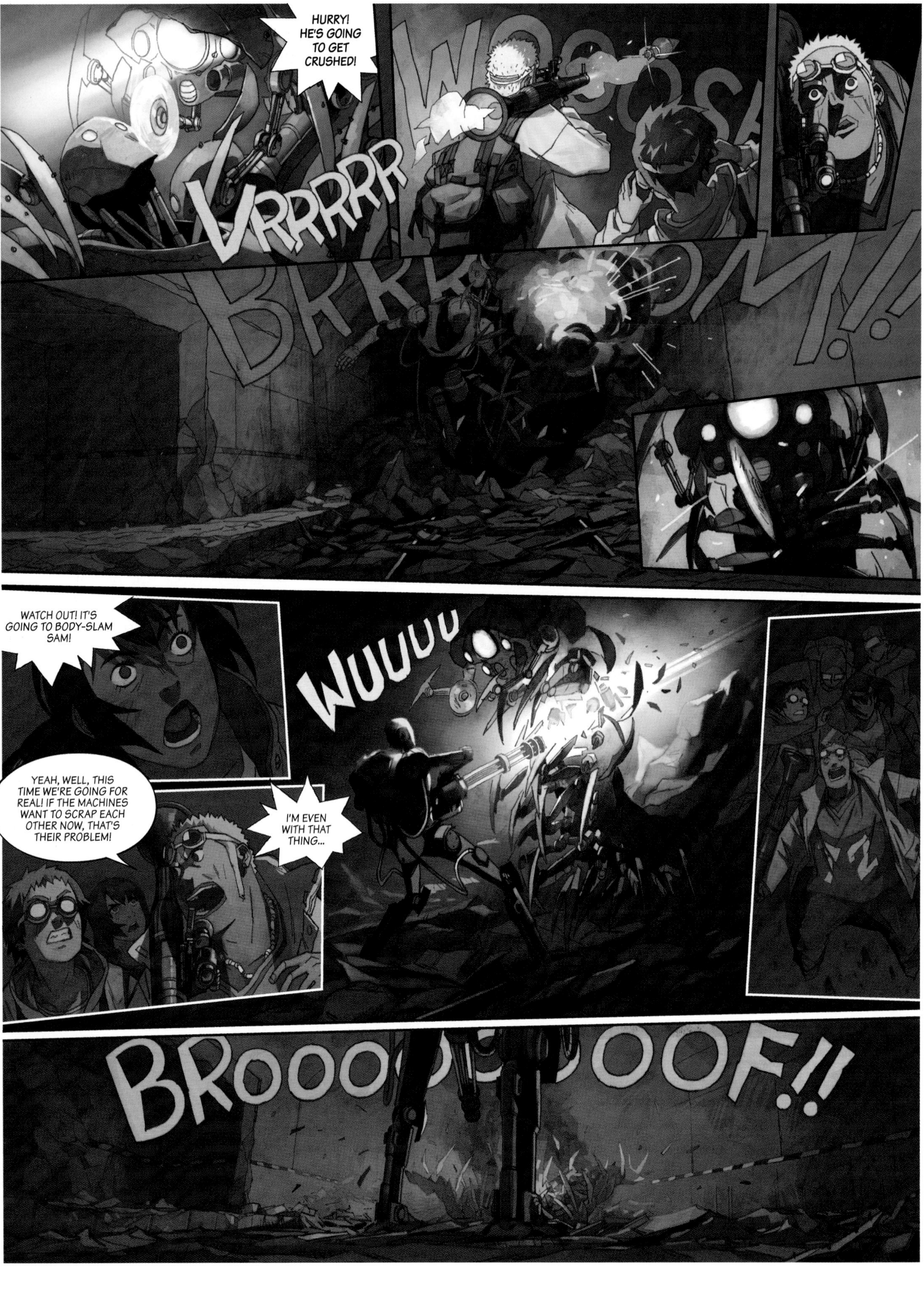
HURRY! HE'S GOING TO GET CRUSHED!
VRRRRR
BRRRROOM!!
WATCH OUT! IT'S GOING TO BODY-SLAM SAM!
WUUUU
YEAH, WELL, THIS TIME WE'RE GOING FOR REAL! IF THE MACHINES WANT TO SCRAP EACH OTHER NOW, THAT'S THEIR PROBLEM!
I'M EVEN WITH THAT THING...
BROOOOOOOOF!!

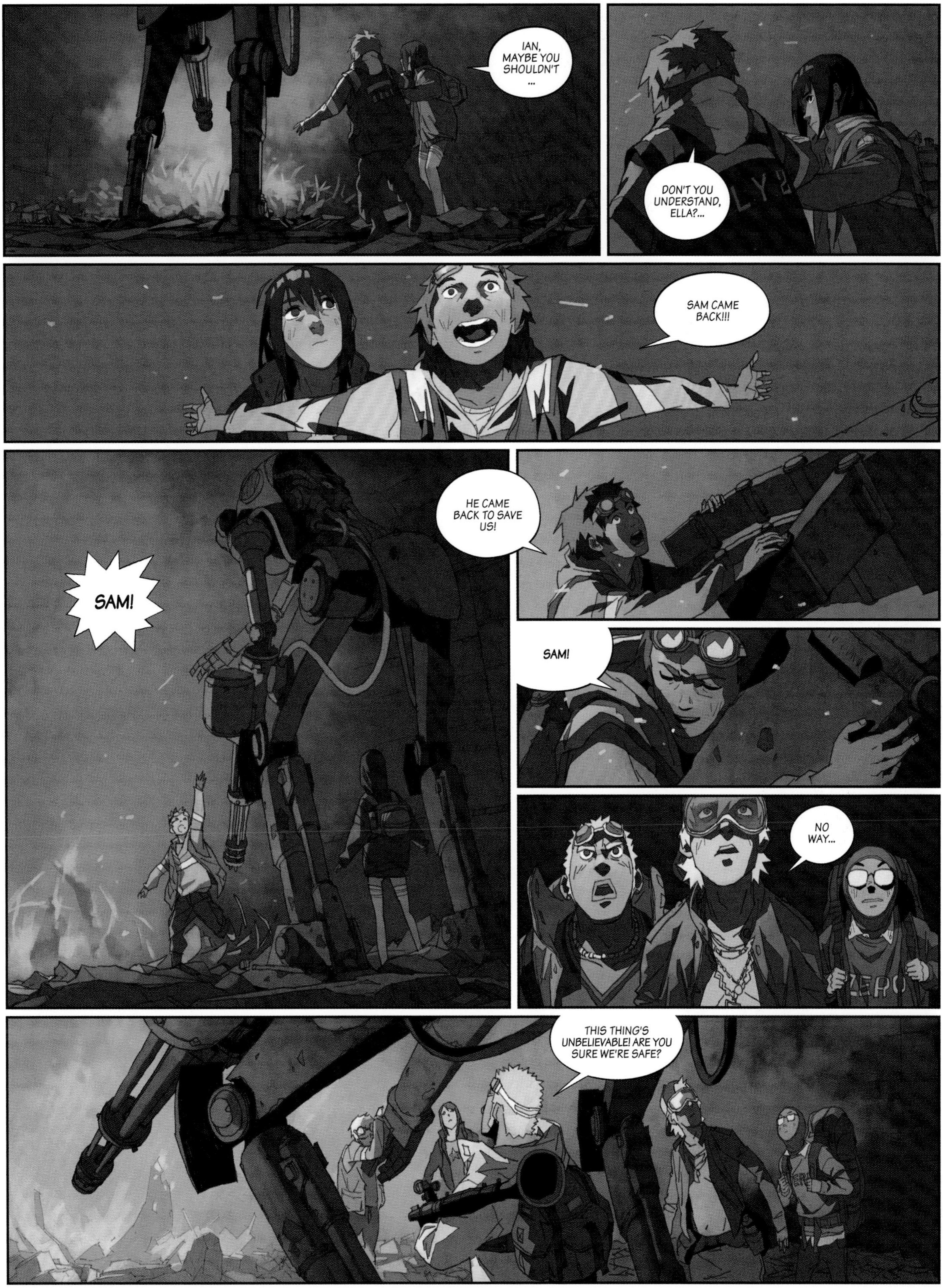
IAN, MAYBE YOU SHOULDN'T ...
DON'T YOU UNDERSTAND, ELLA?...
SAM CAME BACK!!!
SAM!
HE CAME BACK TO SAVE US!
SAM!
NO WAY...
THIS THING'S UNBELIEVABLE! ARE YOU SURE WE'RE SAFE?

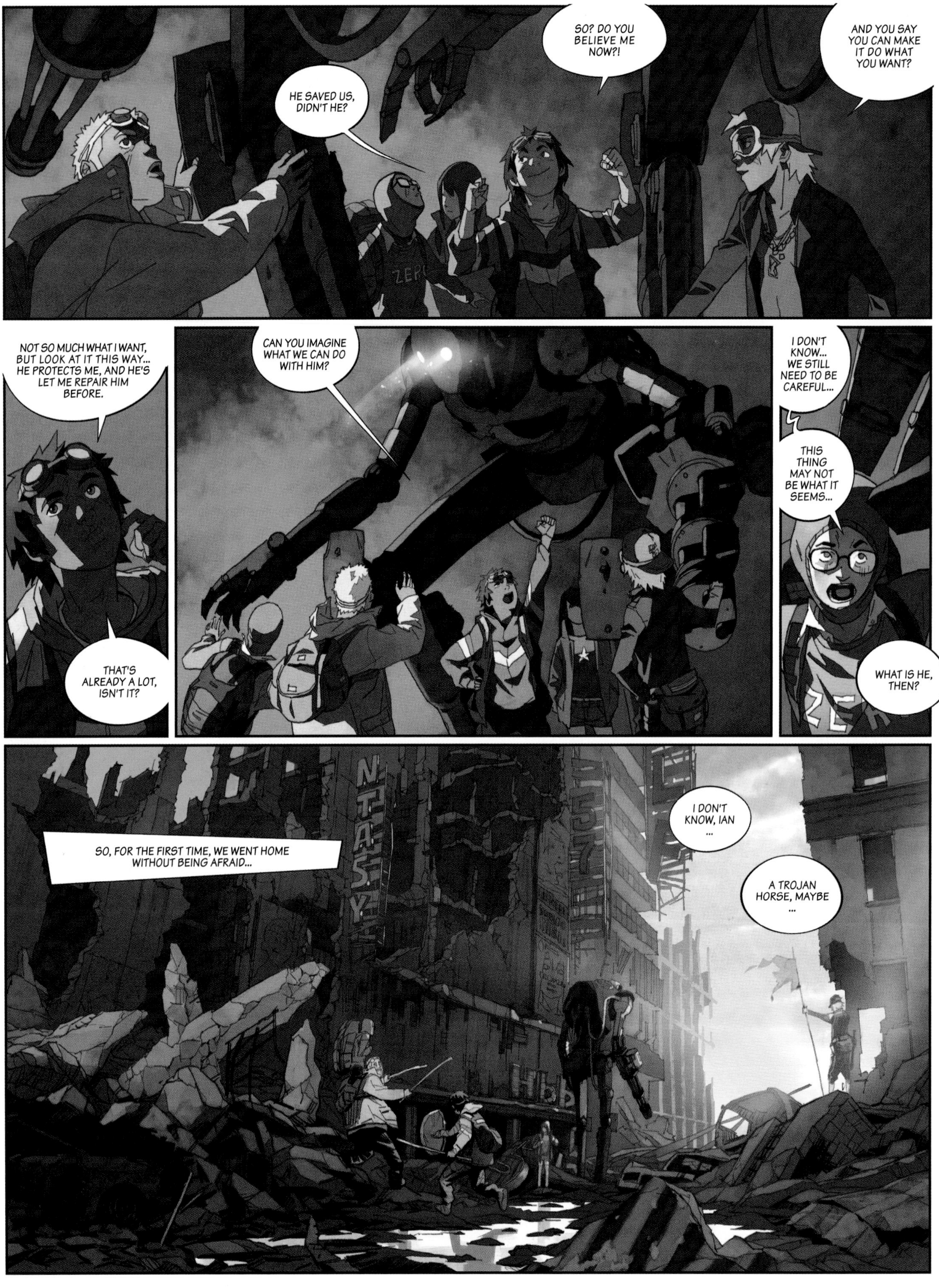
HE SAVED US, DIDN'T HE?
SO? DO YOU BELIEVE ME NOW?!
AND YOU SAY YOU CAN MAKE IT DO WHAT YOU WANT?
NOT SO MUCH WHAT I WANT, BUT LOOK AT IT THIS WAY... HE PROTECTS ME, AND HE'S LET ME REPAIR HIM BEFORE.
THAT'S ALREADY A LOT, ISN'T IT?
CAN YOU IMAGINE WHAT WE CAN DO WITH HIM?
I DON'T KNOW... WE STILL NEED TO BE CAREFUL...
THIS THING MAY NOT BE WHAT IT SEEMS...
WHAT IS HE, THEN?
SO, FOR THE FIRST TIME, WE WENT HOME WITHOUT BEING AFRAID...
I DON'T KNOW, IAN ...
A TROJAN HORSE, MAYBE ...

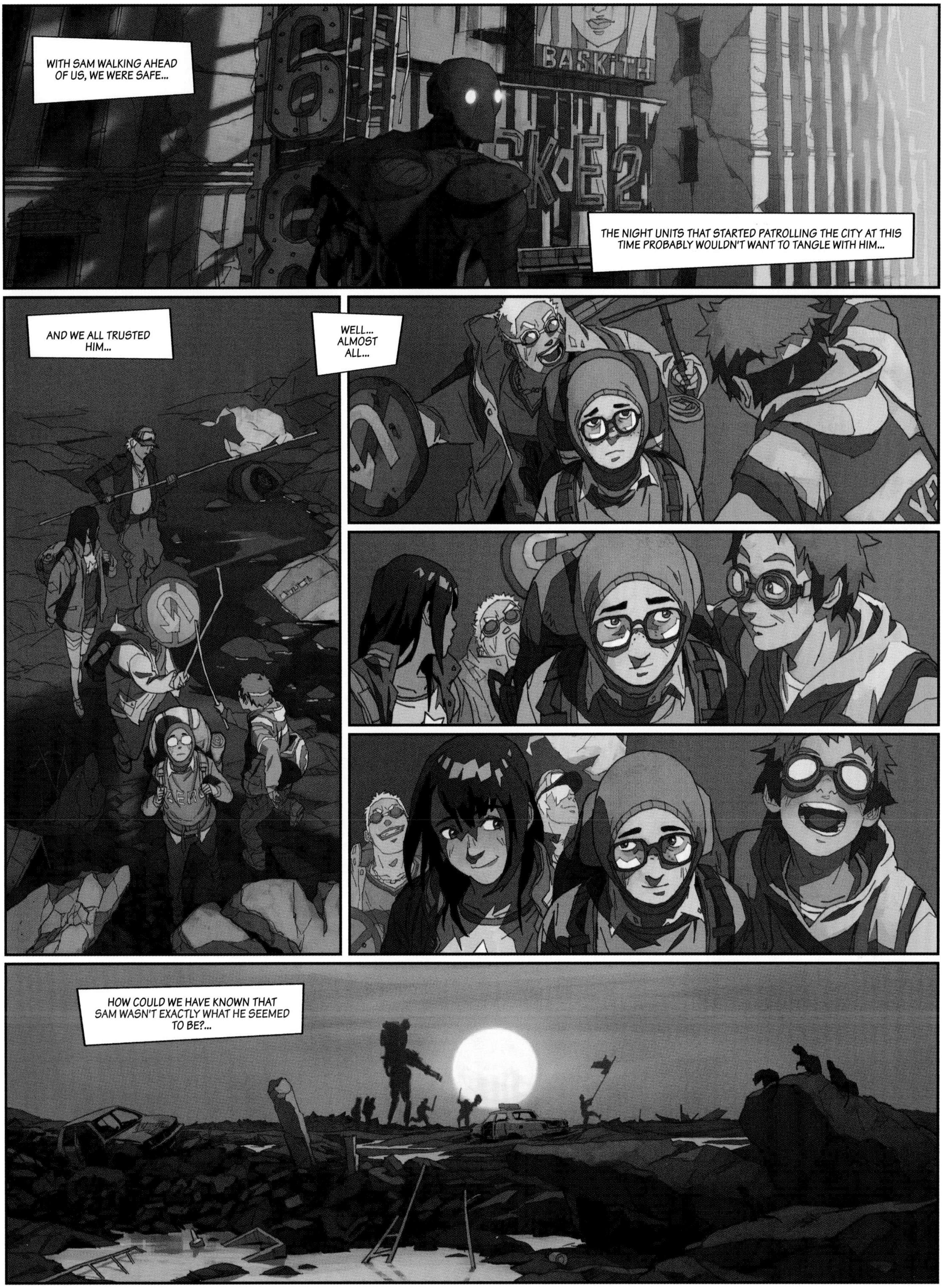
WITH SAM WALKING AHEAD OF US, WE WERE SAFE...
BASKITH
THE NIGHT UNITS THAT STARTED PATROLLING THE CITY AT THIS TIME PROBABLY WOULDN'T WANT TO TANGLE WITH HIM...
AND WE ALL TRUSTED HIM...
WELL... ALMOST ALL...
HOW COULD WE HAVE KNOWN THAT SAM WASN'T EXACTLY WHAT HE SEEMED TO BE?...

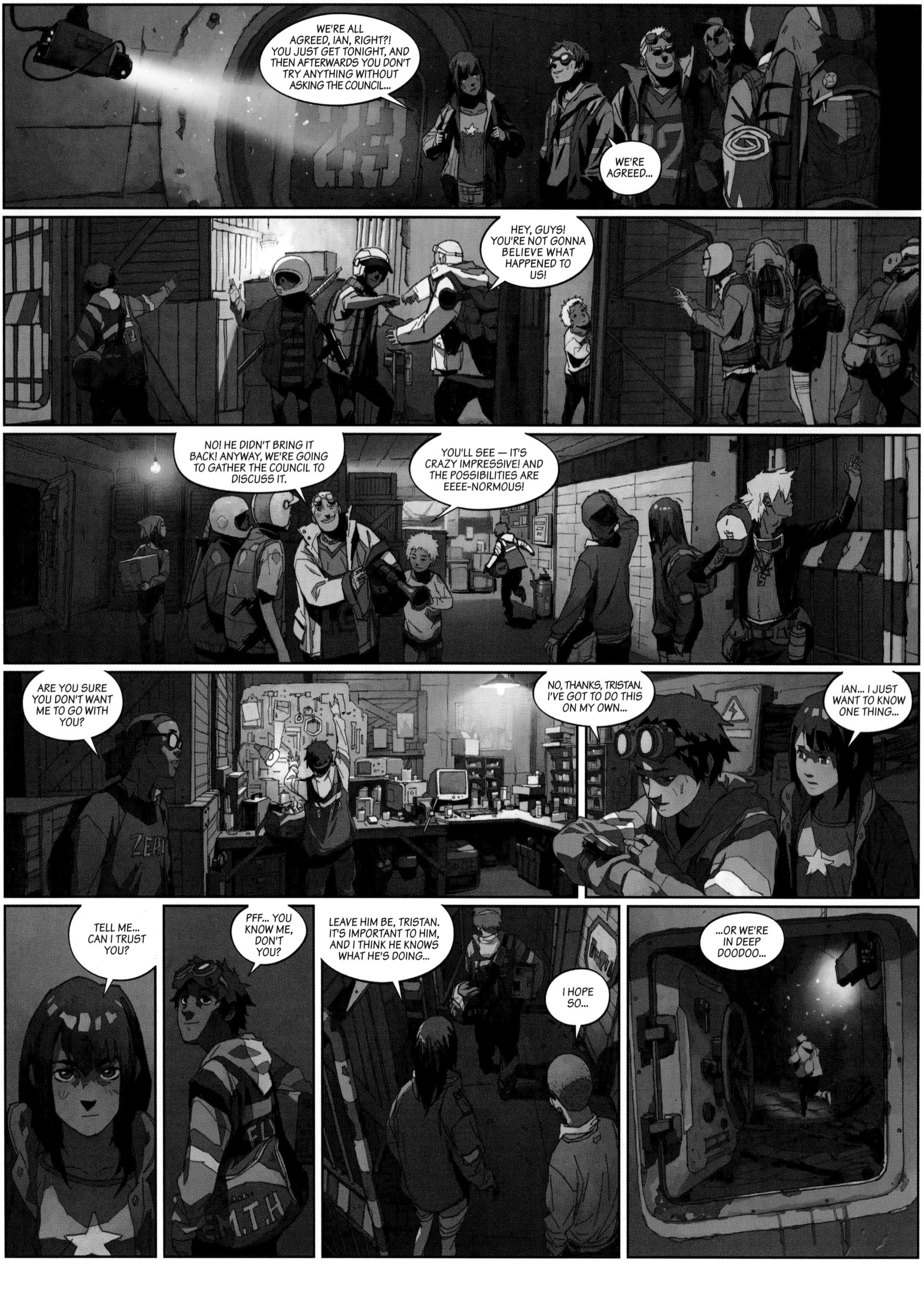
WE'RE ALL AGREED, IAN, RIGHT?! YOU JUST GET TONIGHT, AND THEN AFTERWARDS YOU DON'T TRY ANYTHING WITHOUT ASKING THE COUNCIL...
WE'RE AGREED...
HEY, GUYS! YOU'RE NOT GONNA BELIEVE WHAT HAPPENED TO US!
NO! HE DIDN'T BRING IT BACK! ANYWAY, WE'RE GOING TO GATHER THE COUNCIL TO DISCUSS IT.
YOU'LL SEE — IT'S CRAZY IMPRESSIVE! AND THE POSSIBILITIES ARE EEEE-NORMOUS!
ARE YOU SURE YOU DON'T WANT ME TO GO WITH YOU?
NO, THANKS, TRISTAN. I'VE GOT TO DO THIS ON MY OWN...
IAN... I JUST WANT TO KNOW ONE THING...
TELL ME... CAN I TRUST YOU?
PFF... YOU KNOW ME, DON'T YOU?
LEAVE HIM BE, TRISTAN. IT'S IMPORTANT TO HIM, AND I THINK HE KNOWS WHAT HE'S DOING...
I HOPE SO...
...OR WE'RE IN DEEP DOODOO...

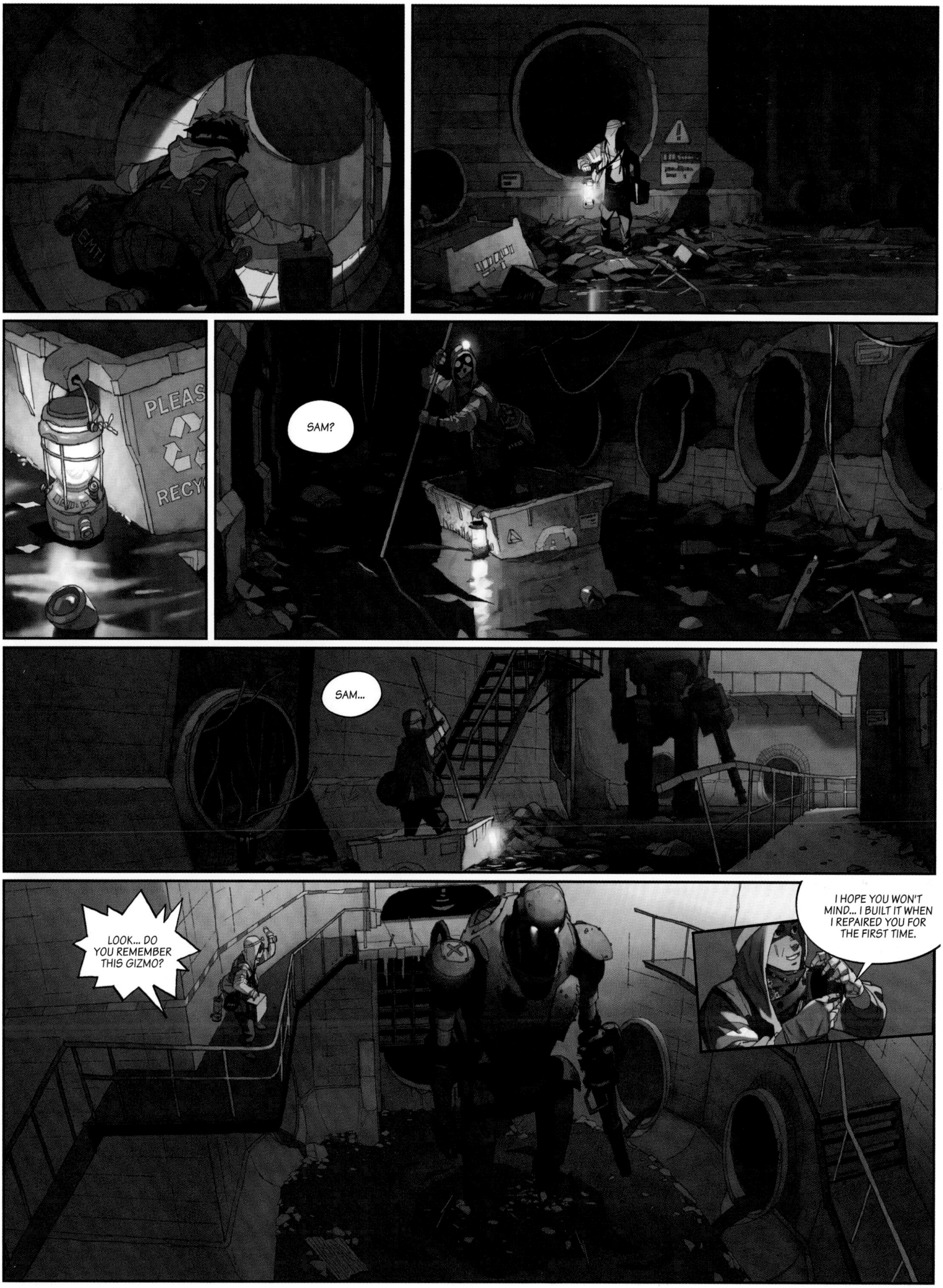
PLEAS
RECYC
SAM?
SAM...
LOOK... DO YOU REMEMBER THIS GIZMO?
I HOPE YOU WON'T MIND... I BUILT IT WHEN I REPAIRED YOU FOR THE FIRST TIME.

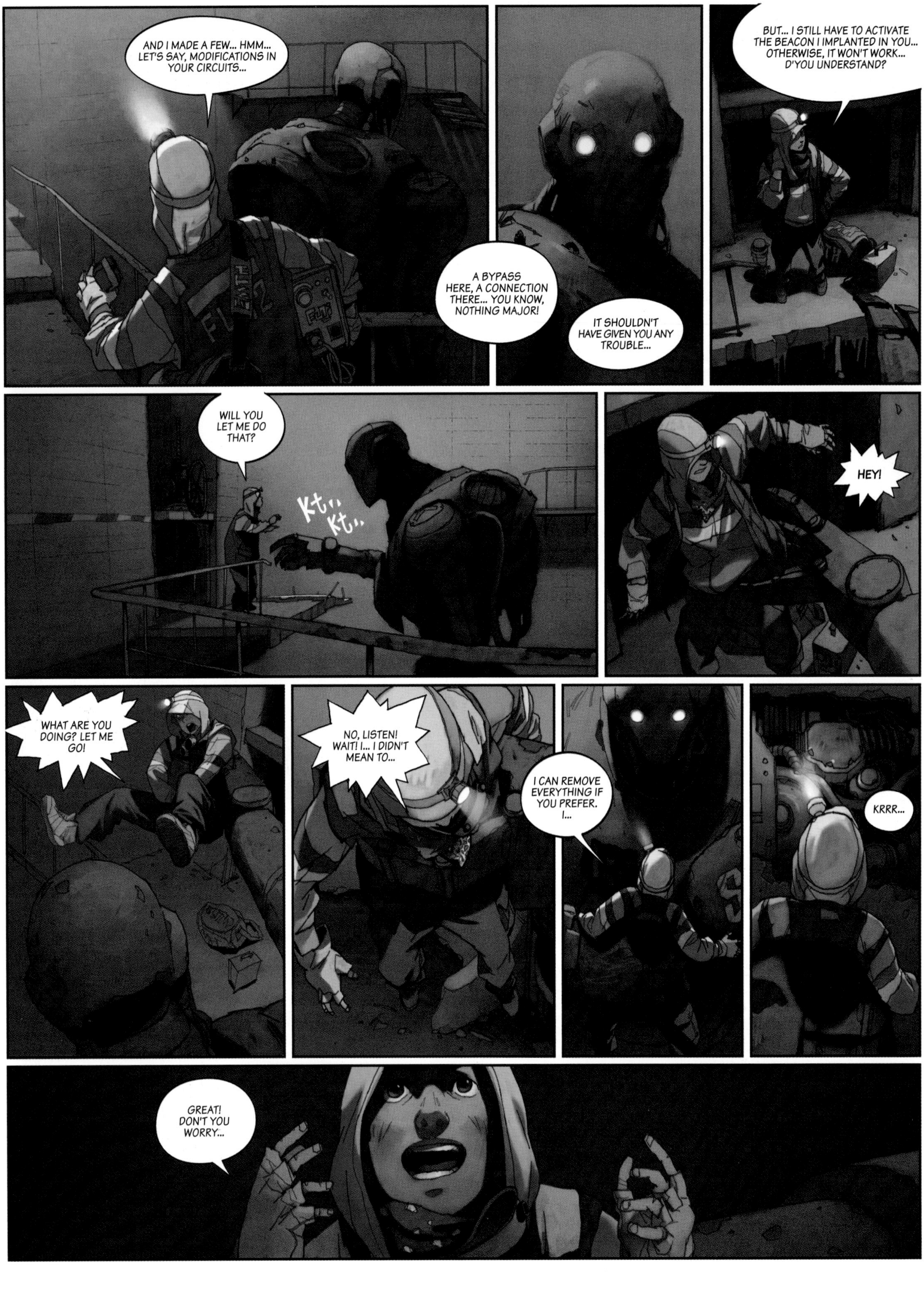
AND I MADE A FEW... HMM... LET'S SAY, MODIFICATIONS IN YOUR CIRCUITS...
A BYPASS HERE, A CONNECTION THERE... YOU KNOW, NOTHING MAJOR!
IT SHOULDN'T HAVE GIVEN YOU ANY TROUBLE...
BUT... I STILL HAVE TO ACTIVATE THE BEACON I IMPLANTED IN YOU... OTHERWISE, IT WON'T WORK... D'YOU UNDERSTAND?
WILL YOU LET ME DO THAT?
Kt.. Kt..
HEY!
WHAT ARE YOU DOING? LET ME GO!
NO, LISTEN! WAIT! I... I DIDN'T MEAN TO...
I CAN REMOVE EVERYTHING IF YOU PREFER. I...
KRRR...
GREAT! DON'T YOU WORRY...

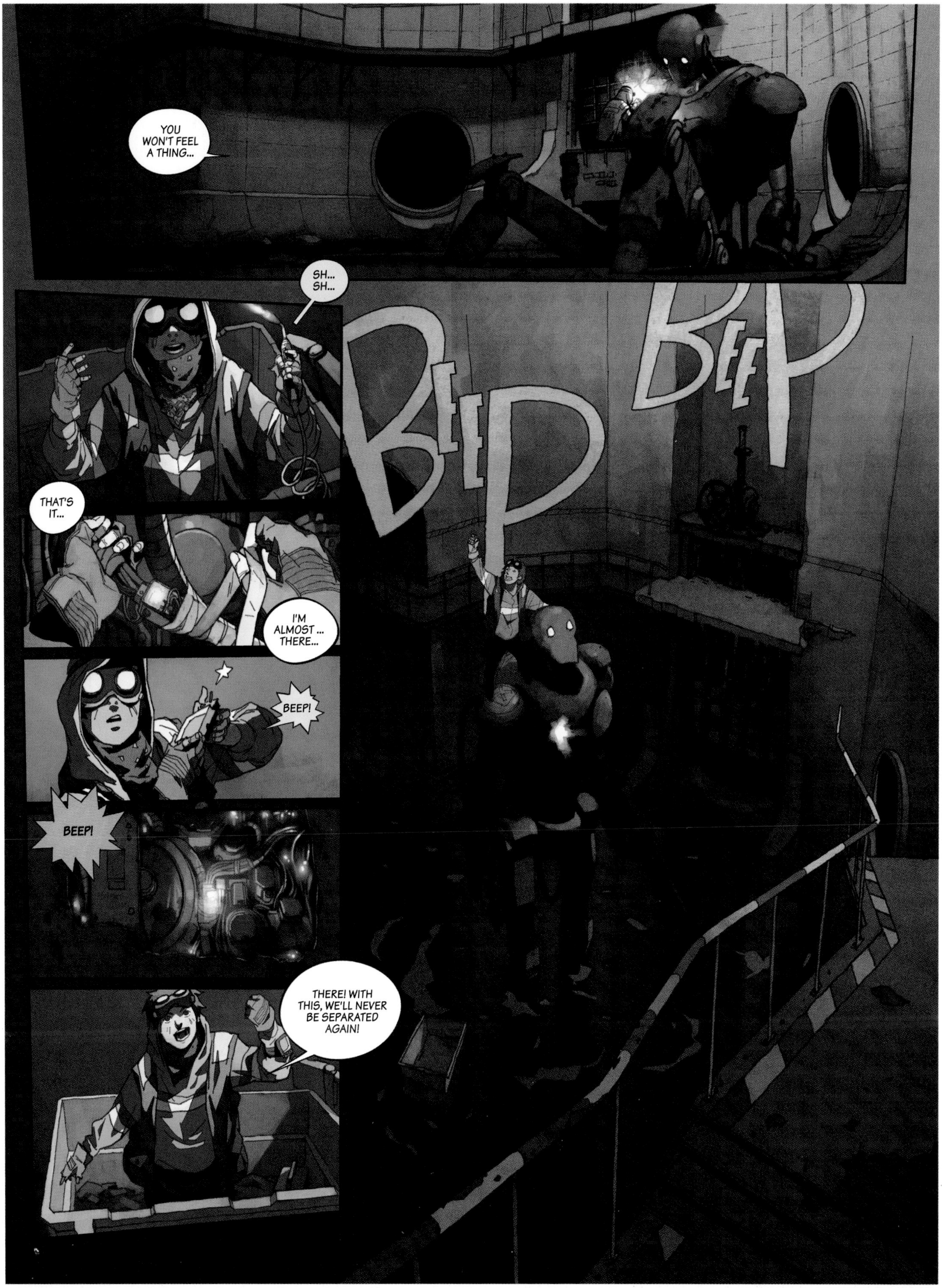
YOU WON'T FEEL A THING...
SH... SH...
BEEP
BEEP
THAT'S IT...
I'M ALMOST ... THERE...
BEEP!
BEEP!
THERE! WITH THIS, WE'LL NEVER BE SEPARATED AGAIN!

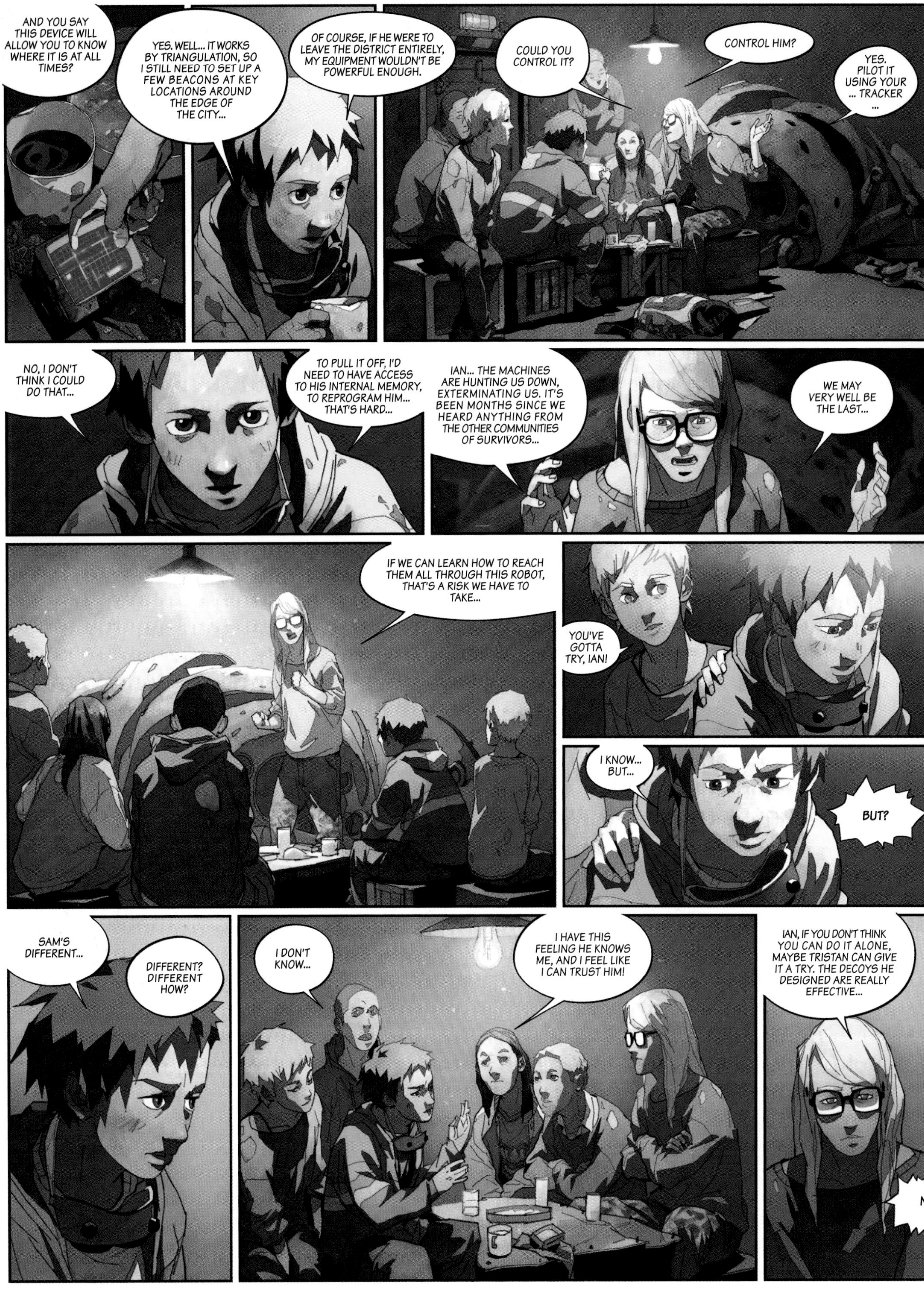
AND YOU SAY THIS DEVICE WILL ALLOW YOU TO KNOW WHERE IT IS AT ALL TIMES?
YES. WELL... IT WORKS BY TRIANGULATION, SO I STILL NEED TO SET UP A FEW BEACONS AT KEY LOCATIONS AROUND THE EDGE OF THE CITY...
OF COURSE, IF HE WERE TO LEAVE THE DISTRICT ENTIRELY, MY EQUIPMENT WOULDN'T BE POWERFUL ENOUGH.
COULD YOU CONTROL IT?
CONTROL HIM?
YES. PILOT IT USING YOUR ... TRACKER ...
NO, I DON'T THINK I COULD DO THAT...
TO PULL IT OFF, I'D NEED TO HAVE ACCESS TO HIS INTERNAL MEMORY, TO REPROGRAM HIM... THAT'S HARD...
IAN... THE MACHINES ARE HUNTING US DOWN, EXTERMINATING US. IT'S BEEN MONTHS SINCE WE HEARD ANYTHING FROM THE OTHER COMMUNITIES OF SURVIVORS...
WE MAY VERY WELL BE THE LAST...
IF WE CAN LEARN HOW TO REACH THEM ALL THROUGH THIS ROBOT, THAT'S A RISK WE HAVE TO TAKE...
YOU'VE GOTTA TRY, IAN!
I KNOW... BUT...
BUT?
SAM'S DIFFERENT...
DIFFERENT? DIFFERENT HOW?
I DON'T KNOW...
I HAVE THIS FEELING HE KNOWS ME, AND I FEEL LIKE I CAN TRUST HIM!
IAN, IF YOU DON'T THINK YOU CAN DO IT ALONE, MAYBE TRISTAN CAN GIVE IT A TRY. THE DECOYS HE DESIGNED ARE REALLY EFFECTIVE...
NO!

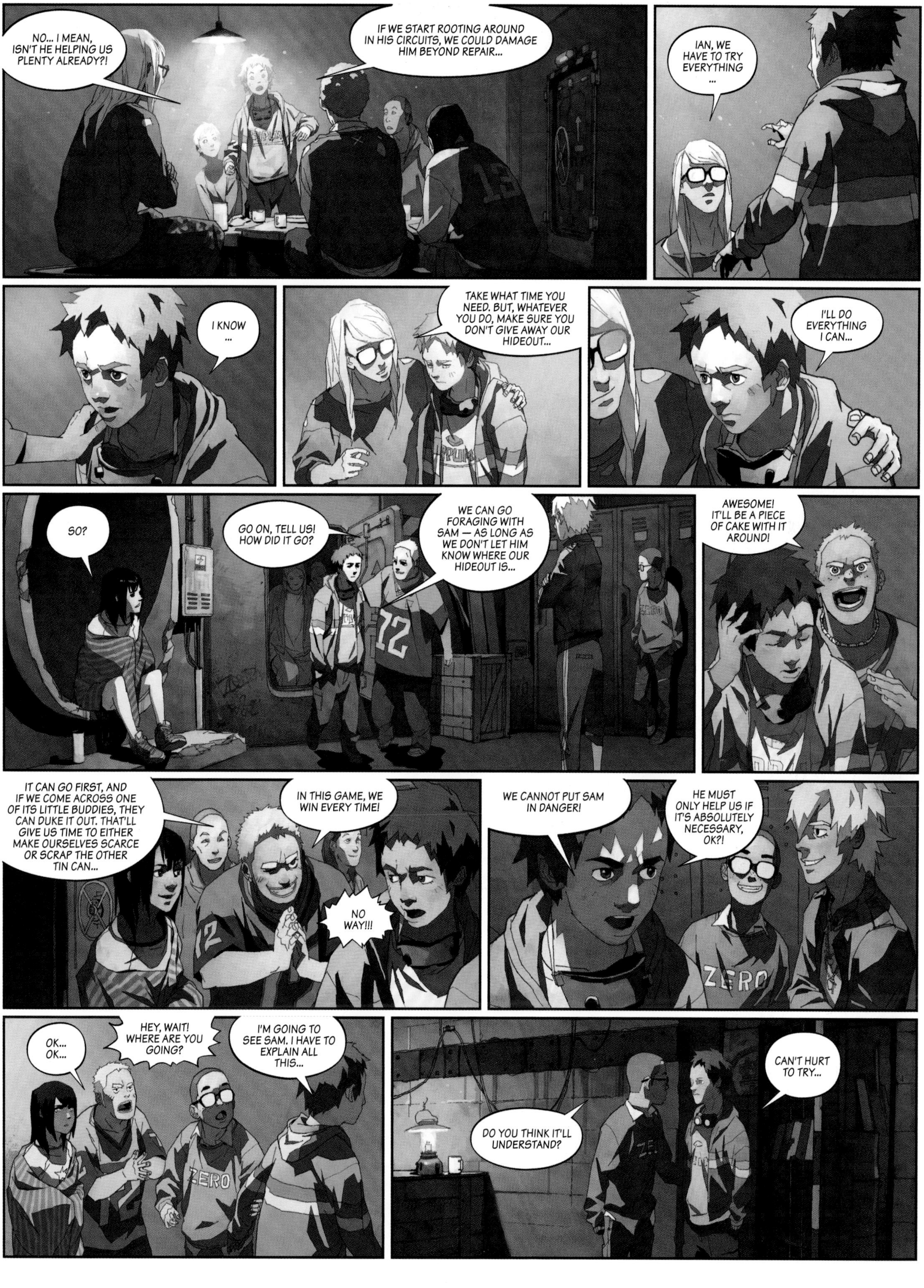
NO... I MEAN, ISN'T HE HELPING US PLENTY ALREADY?!
IF WE START ROOTING AROUND IN HIS CIRCUITS, WE COULD DAMAGE HIM BEYOND REPAIR...
IAN, WE HAVE TO TRY EVERYTHING ...
I KNOW ...
TAKE WHAT TIME YOU NEED. BUT, WHATEVER YOU DO, MAKE SURE YOU DON'T GIVE AWAY OUR HIDEOUT...
I'LL DO EVERYTHING I CAN...
SO?
GO ON, TELL US! HOW DID IT GO?
WE CAN GO FORAGING WITH SAM — AS LONG AS WE DON'T LET HIM KNOW WHERE OUR HIDEOUT IS...
AWESOME! IT'LL BE A PIECE OF CAKE WITH IT AROUND!
IT CAN GO FIRST, AND IF WE COME ACROSS ONE OF ITS LITTLE BUDDIES, THEY CAN DUKE IT OUT. THAT'LL GIVE US TIME TO EITHER MAKE OURSELVES SCARCE OR SCRAP THE OTHER TIN CAN...
IN THIS GAME, WE WIN EVERY TIME!
NO WAY!!!
WE CANNOT PUT SAM IN DANGER!
HE MUST ONLY HELP US IF IT'S ABSOLUTELY NECESSARY, OK?!
OK... OK...
HEY, WAIT! WHERE ARE YOU GOING?
I'M GOING TO SEE SAM. I HAVE TO EXPLAIN ALL THIS...
DO YOU THINK IT'LL UNDERSTAND?
CAN'T HURT TO TRY...

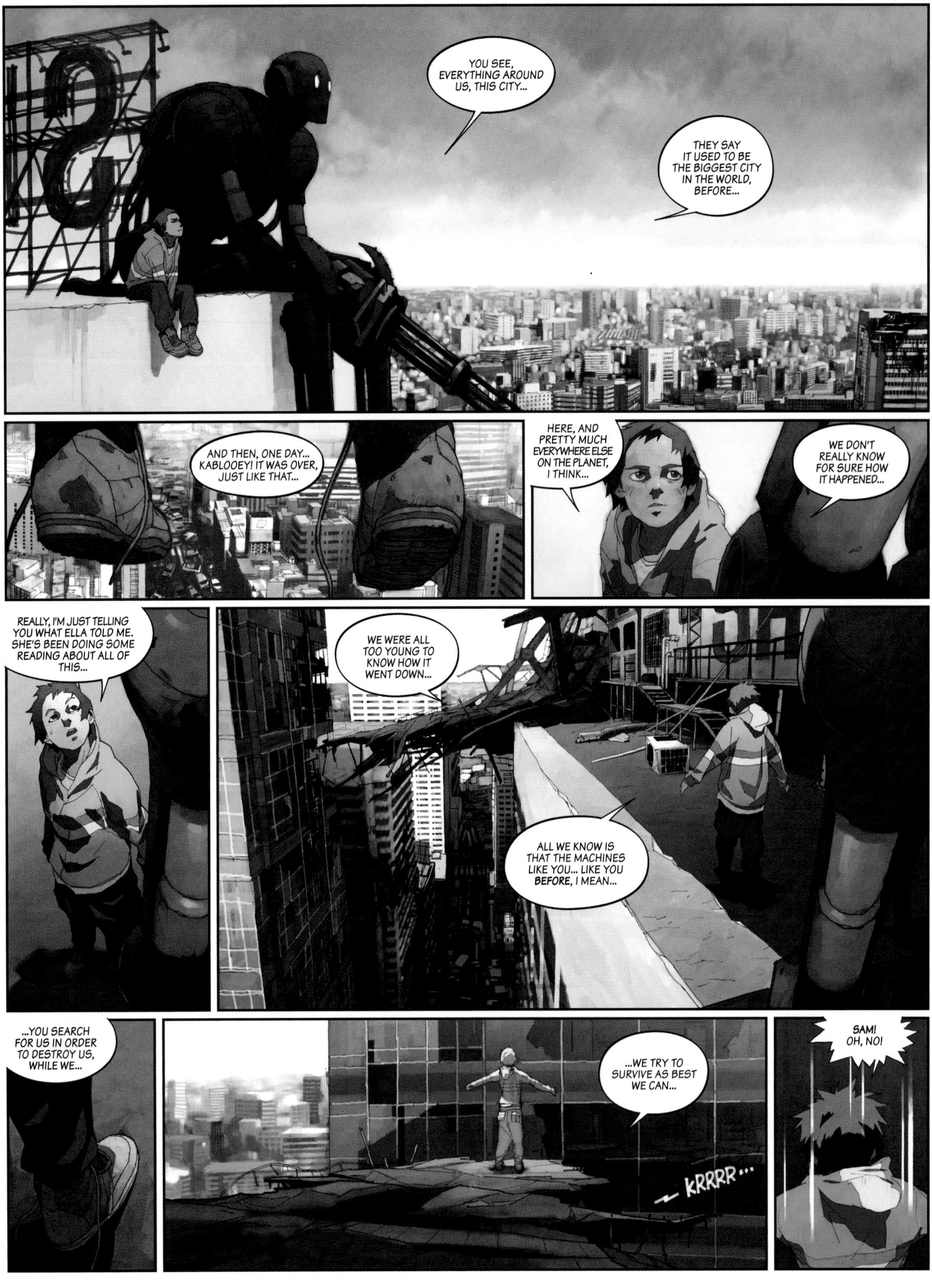
YOU SEE, EVERYTHING AROUND US, THIS CITY...
THEY SAY IT USED TO BE THE BIGGEST CITY IN THE WORLD, BEFORE...
AND THEN, ONE DAY... KABLOOEY! IT WAS OVER, JUST LIKE THAT...
HERE, AND PRETTY MUCH EVERYWHERE ELSE ON THE PLANET, I THINK...
WE DON'T REALLY KNOW FOR SURE HOW IT HAPPENED...
REALLY, I'M JUST TELLING YOU WHAT ELLA TOLD ME. SHE'S BEEN DOING SOME READING ABOUT ALL OF THIS...
WE WERE ALL TOO YOUNG TO KNOW HOW IT WENT DOWN...
ALL WE KNOW IS THAT THE MACHINES LIKE YOU... LIKE YOU **BEFORE**, I MEAN...
...YOU SEARCH FOR US IN ORDER TO DESTROY US, WHILE WE...
...WE TRY TO SURVIVE AS BEST WE CAN...
KRRRR...
SAM! OH, NO!

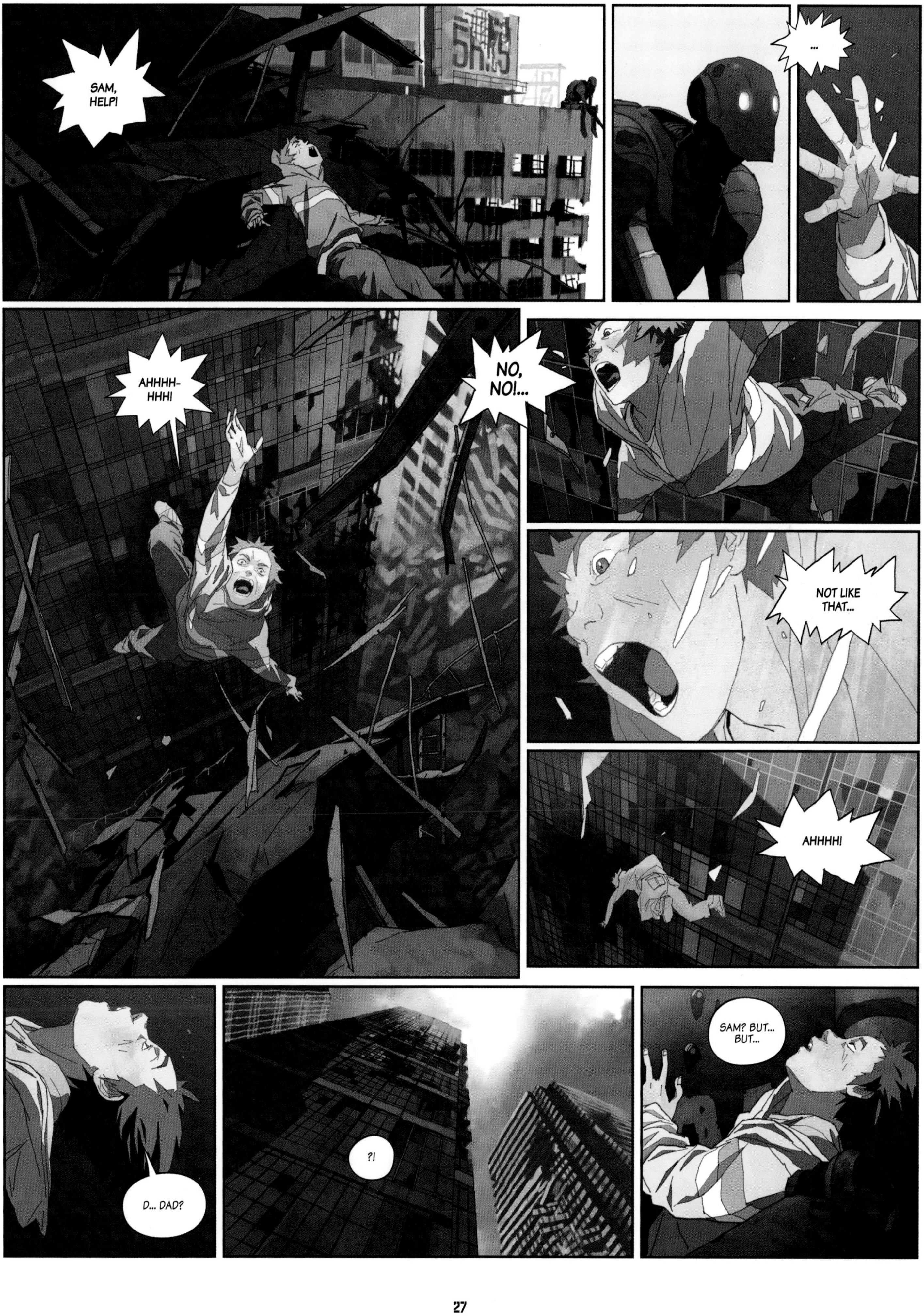
SAM, HELP!
...
AHHHH-HHH!
NO, NO!...
NOT LIKE THAT...
AHHHH!
D... DAD?
?!
SAM? BUT... BUT...

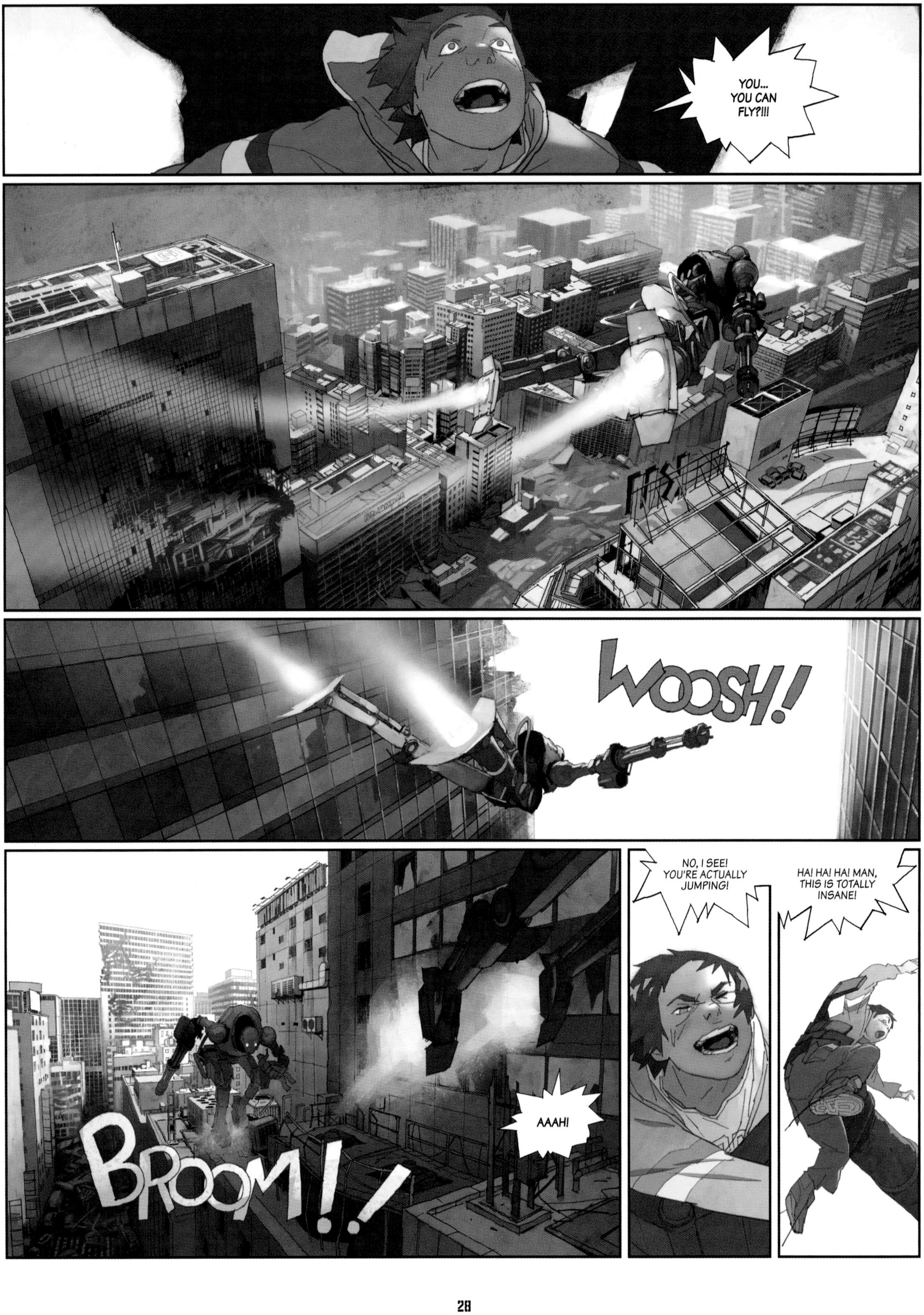
YOU... YOU CAN FLY?!!!
WOOSH!
BROOM!!
AAAH!
NO, I SEE! YOU'RE ACTUALLY JUMPING!
HA! HA! HA! MAN, THIS IS TOTALLY INSANE!

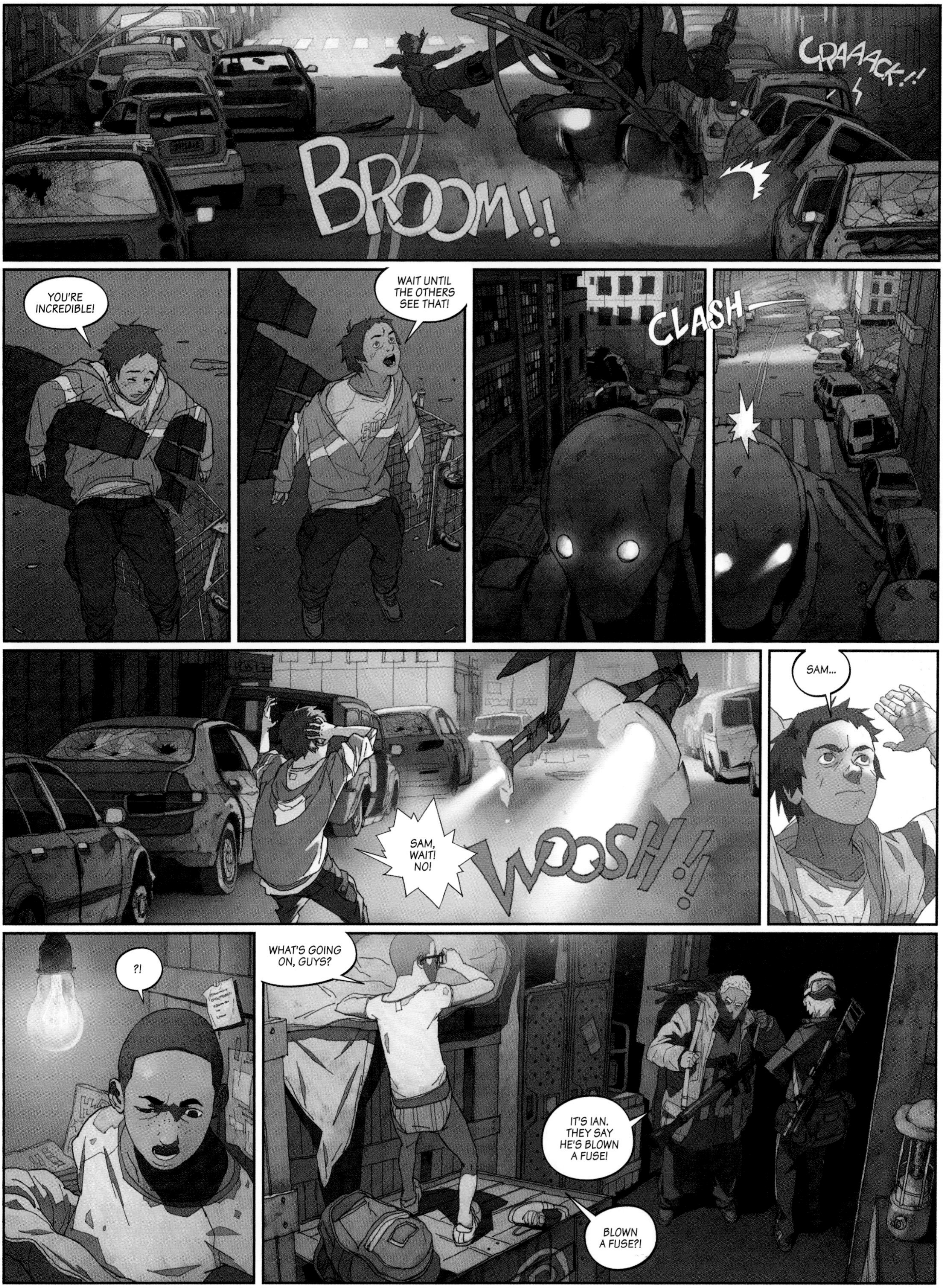
CRAAACK!!
BROOM!!
YOU'RE INCREDIBLE!
WAIT UNTIL THE OTHERS SEE THAT!
CLASH
SAM...
SAM, WAIT! NO!
WOOSH!!
?!
WHAT'S GOING ON, GUYS?
IT'S IAN. THEY SAY HE'S BLOWN A FUSE!
BLOWN A FUSE?!

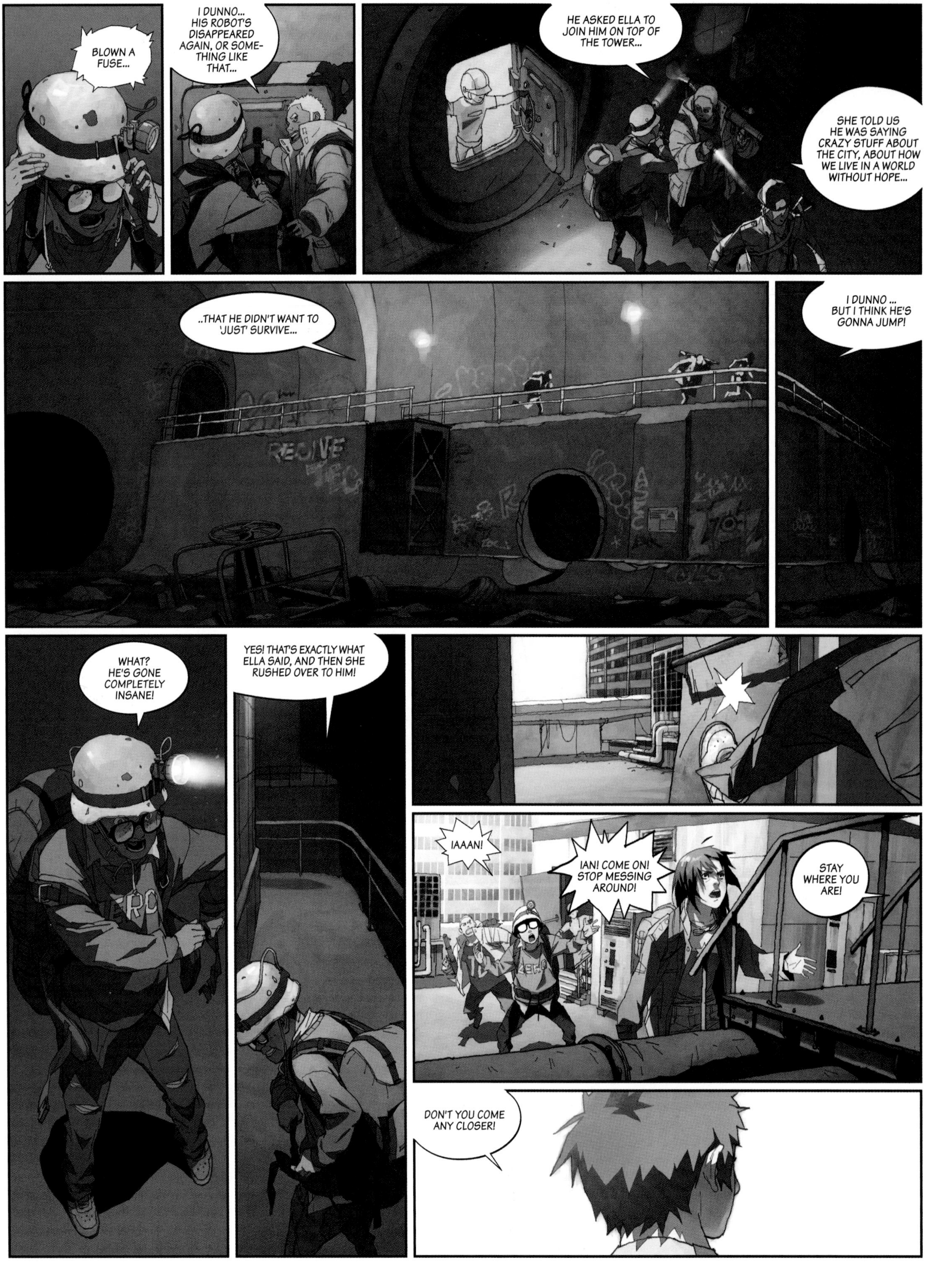
BLOWN A FUSE...
I DUNNO... HIS ROBOT'S DISAPPEARED AGAIN, OR SOME-THING LIKE THAT...
HE ASKED ELLA TO JOIN HIM ON TOP OF THE TOWER...
SHE TOLD US HE WAS SAYING CRAZY STUFF ABOUT THE CITY, ABOUT HOW WE LIVE IN A WORLD WITHOUT HOPE...
..THAT HE DIDN'T WANT TO 'JUST' SURVIVE...
I DUNNO ... BUT I THINK HE'S GONNA JUMP!
WHAT? HE'S GONE COMPLETELY INSANE!
YES! THAT'S EXACTLY WHAT ELLA SAID, AND THEN SHE RUSHED OVER TO HIM!
IAAAN!
IAN! COME ON! STOP MESSING AROUND!
STAY WHERE YOU ARE!
DON'T YOU COME ANY CLOSER!

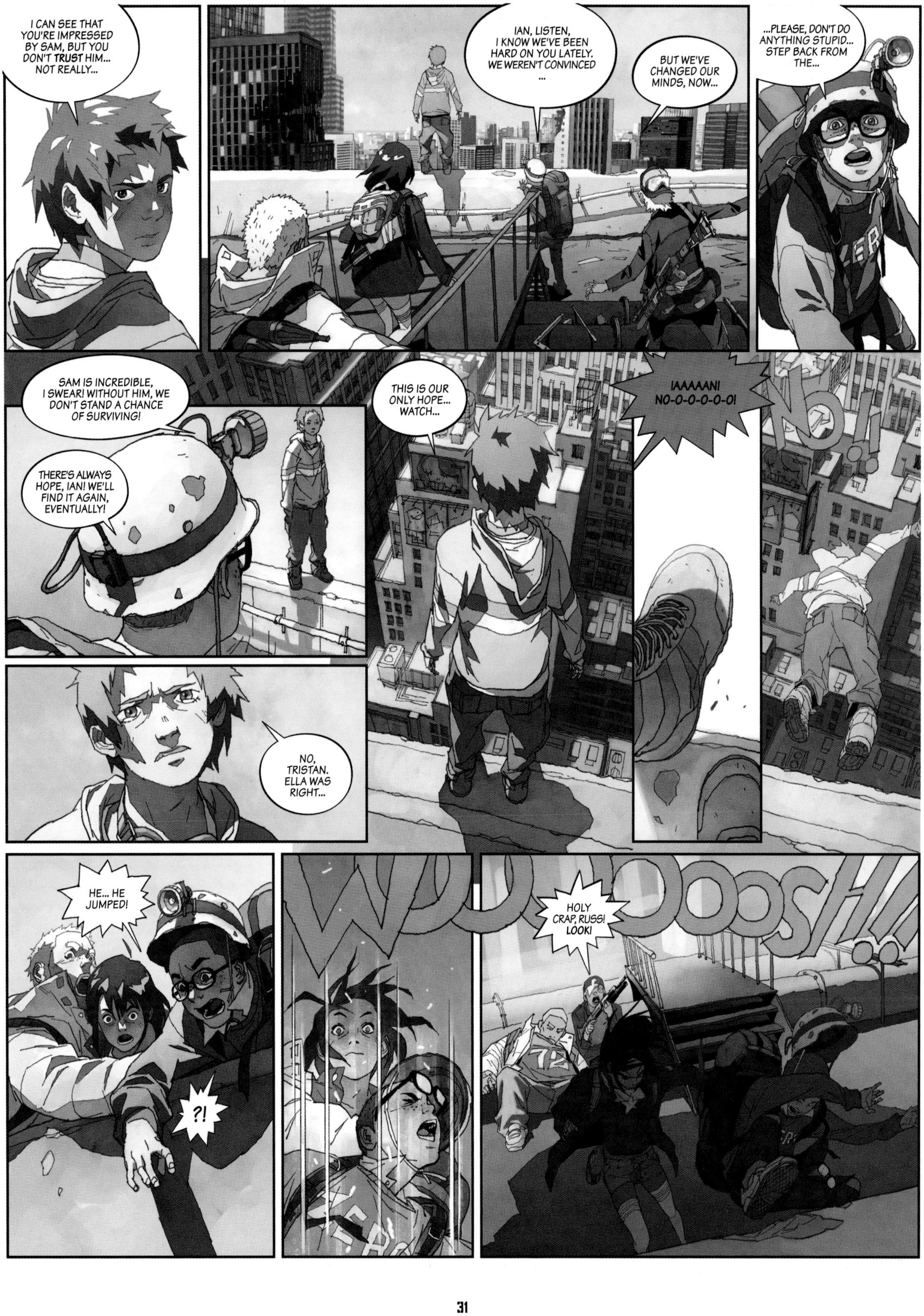
I CAN SEE THAT YOU'RE IMPRESSED BY SAM, BUT YOU DON'T **TRUST** HIM... NOT REALLY...
IAN, LISTEN, I KNOW WE'VE BEEN HARD ON YOU LATELY. WE WEREN'T CONVINCED ...
BUT WE'VE CHANGED OUR MINDS, NOW...
...PLEASE, DON'T DO ANYTHING STUPID... STEP BACK FROM THE...
SAM IS INCREDIBLE, I SWEAR! WITHOUT HIM, WE DON'T STAND A CHANCE OF SURVIVING!
THERE'S ALWAYS HOPE, IAN! WE'LL FIND IT AGAIN, EVENTUALLY!
NO, TRISTAN. ELLA WAS RIGHT...
THIS IS OUR ONLY HOPE... WATCH...
¡AAAAAN! NO-O-O-O-O-O!
NO!!
HE... HE JUMPED!
?!
WOOOOOSH!!
HOLY CRAP, RUSS! **LOOK!**

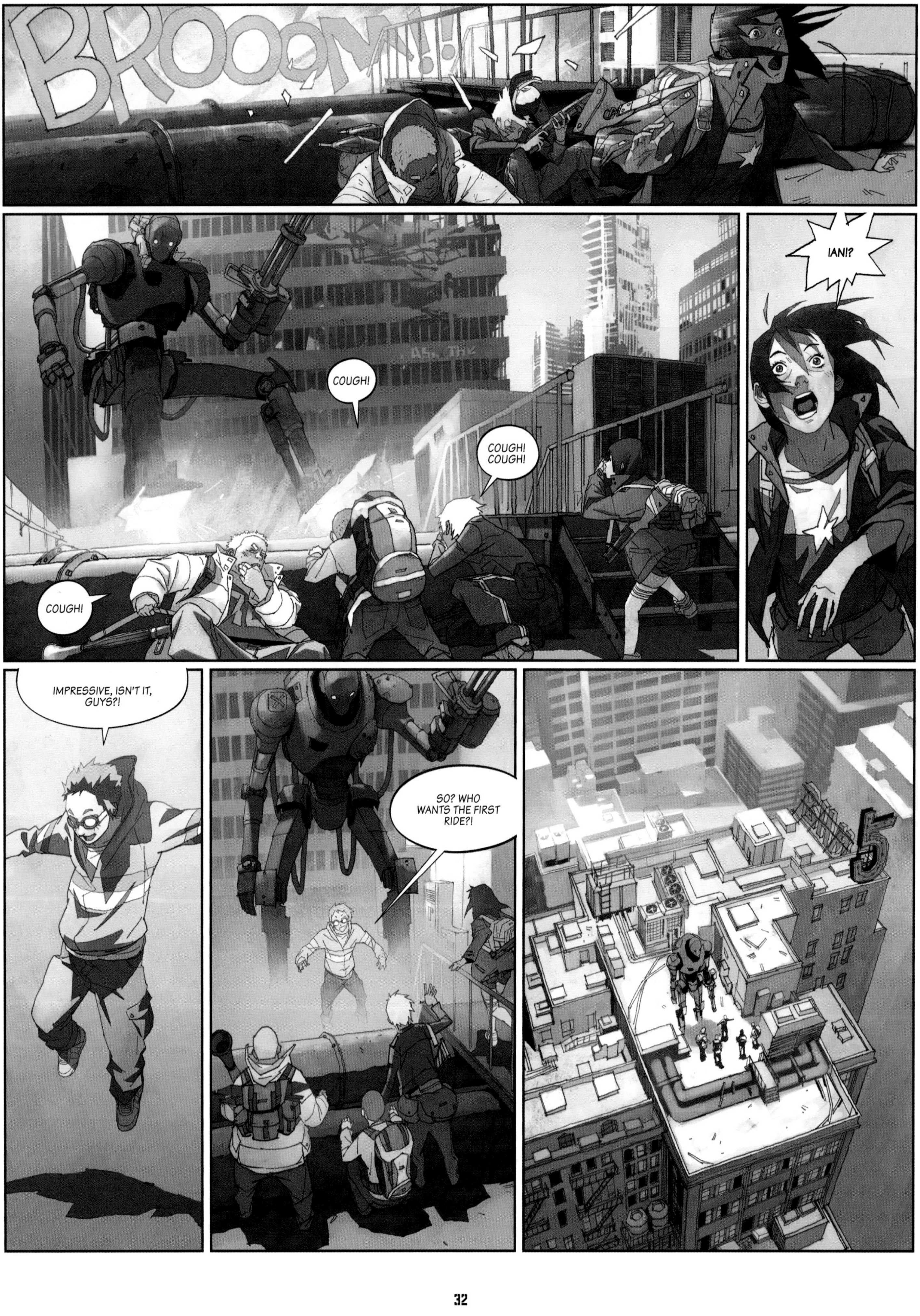
BROOOM!!
COUGH!
COUGH! COUGH!
COUGH!
IAN!?
IMPRESSIVE, ISN'T IT, GUYS?!
SO? WHO WANTS THE FIRST RIDE?!

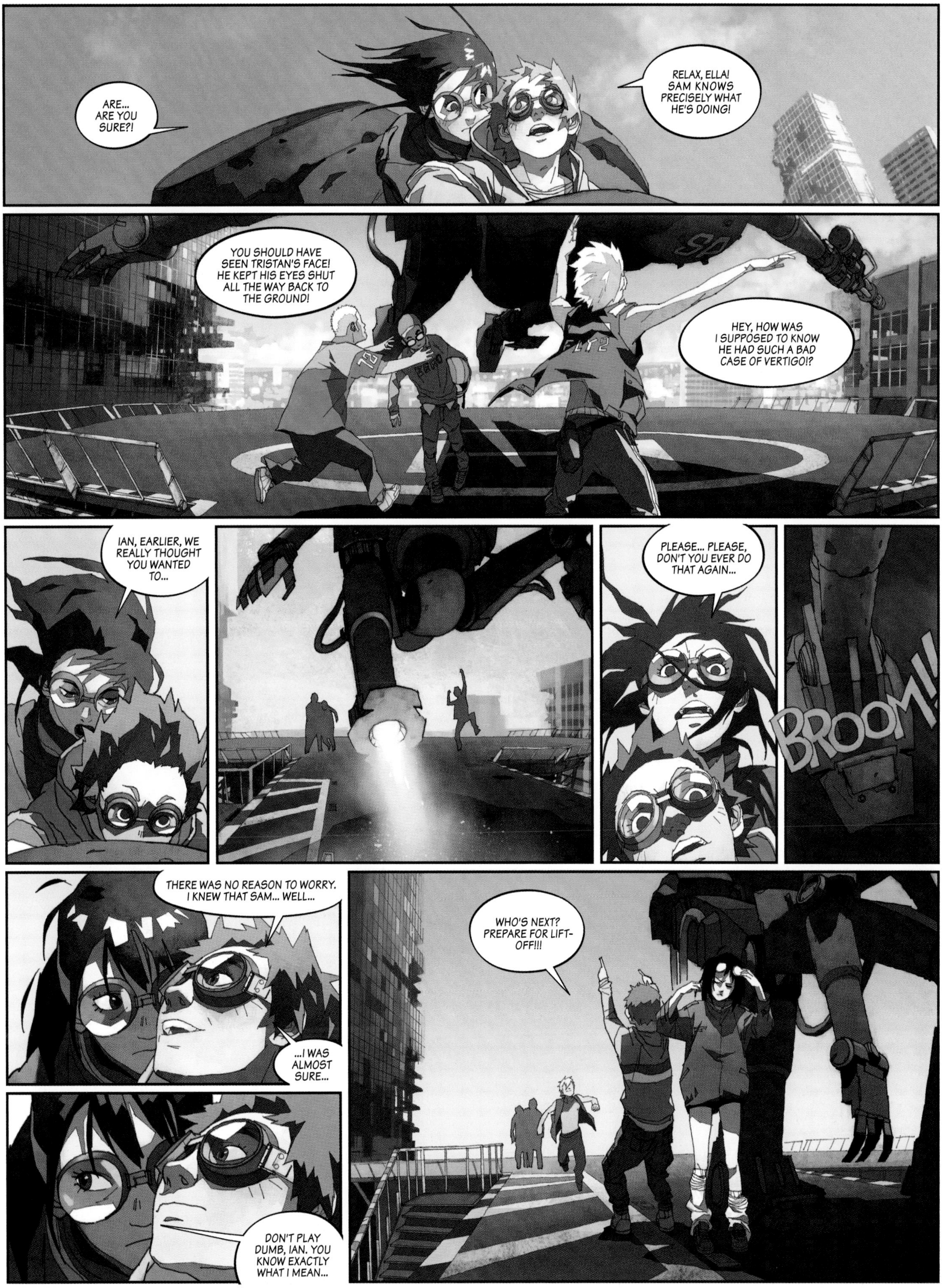

ARE... ARE YOU SURE?!
RELAX, ELLA! SAM KNOWS PRECISELY WHAT HE'S DOING!
YOU SHOULD HAVE SEEN TRISTAN'S FACE! HE KEPT HIS EYES SHUT ALL THE WAY BACK TO THE GROUND!
HEY, HOW WAS I SUPPOSED TO KNOW HE HAD SUCH A BAD CASE OF VERTIGO!?
IAN, EARLIER, WE REALLY THOUGHT YOU WANTED TO...
PLEASE... PLEASE, DON'T YOU EVER DO THAT AGAIN...
BROOM!!
THERE WAS NO REASON TO WORRY. I KNEW THAT SAM... WELL...
...I WAS ALMOST SURE...
DON'T PLAY DUMB, IAN. YOU KNOW EXACTLY WHAT I MEAN...
WHO'S NEXT? PREPARE FOR LIFT-OFF!!!

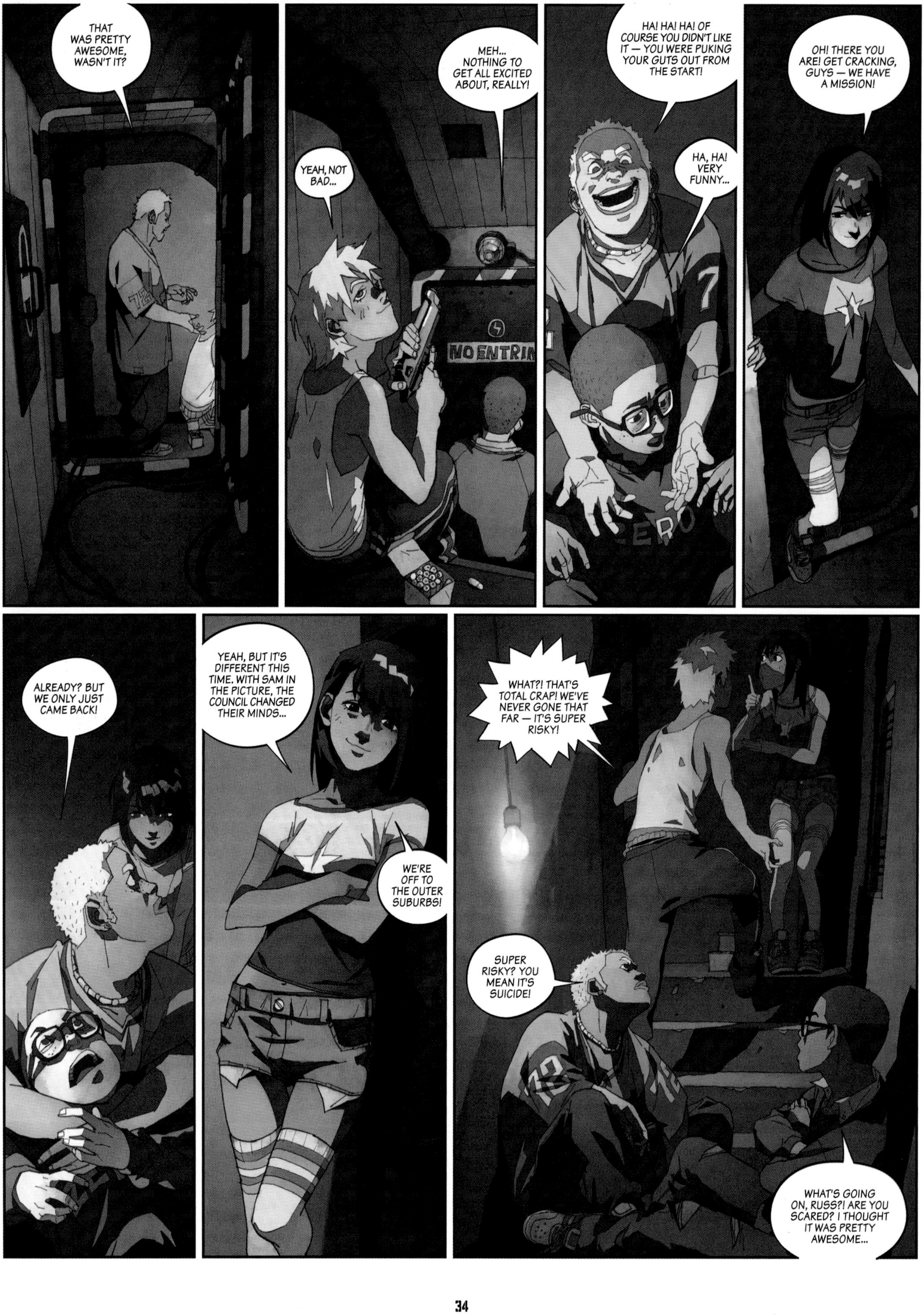
THAT WAS PRETTY AWESOME, WASN'T IT?
MEH... NOTHING TO GET ALL EXCITED ABOUT, REALLY!
YEAH, NOT BAD...
NO ENTRI
HA! HA! HA! OF COURSE YOU DIDN'T LIKE IT — YOU WERE PUKING YOUR GUTS OUT FROM THE START!
HA, HA! VERY FUNNY...
OH! THERE YOU ARE! GET CRACKING, GUYS — WE HAVE A MISSION!
ALREADY? BUT WE ONLY JUST CAME BACK!
YEAH, BUT IT'S DIFFERENT THIS TIME. WITH SAM IN THE PICTURE, THE COUNCIL CHANGED THEIR MINDS...
WE'RE OFF TO THE OUTER SUBURBS!
WHAT?! THAT'S TOTAL CRAP! WE'VE NEVER GONE THAT FAR — IT'S SUPER RISKY!
SUPER RISKY? YOU MEAN IT'S SUICIDE!
WHAT'S GOING ON, RUSS?! ARE YOU SCARED? I THOUGHT IT WAS PRETTY AWESOME...

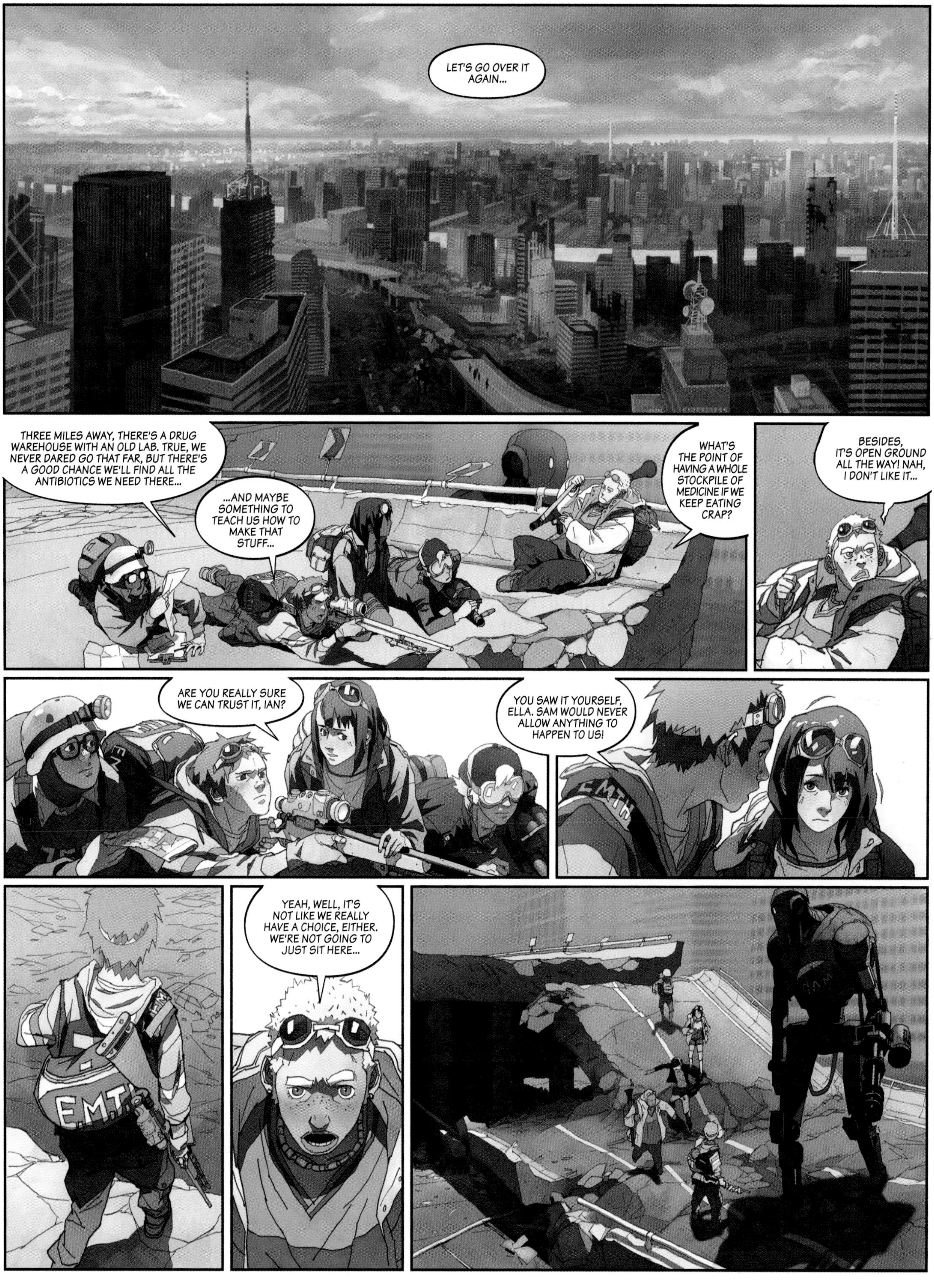
LET'S GO OVER IT AGAIN...
THREE MILES AWAY, THERE'S A DRUG WAREHOUSE WITH AN OLD LAB. TRUE, WE NEVER DARED GO THAT FAR, BUT THERE'S A GOOD CHANCE WE'LL FIND ALL THE ANTIBIOTICS WE NEED THERE...
...AND MAYBE SOMETHING TO TEACH US HOW TO MAKE THAT STUFF...
WHAT'S THE POINT OF HAVING A WHOLE STOCKPILE OF MEDICINE IF WE KEEP EATING CRAP?
BESIDES, IT'S OPEN GROUND ALL THE WAY! NAH, I DON'T LIKE IT...
ARE YOU REALLY SURE WE CAN TRUST IT, IAN?
YOU SAW IT YOURSELF, ELLA. SAM WOULD NEVER ALLOW ANYTHING TO HAPPEN TO US!
YEAH, WELL, IT'S NOT LIKE WE REALLY HAVE A CHOICE, EITHER. WE'RE NOT GOING TO JUST SIT HERE...

MAN, THIS AREA GOT HAMMERED HARD! ARE YOU SURE WE'LL FIND ANYTHING USABLE HERE?

WE'D BETTER, RUSS. WE'RE TAKING ENOUGH RISKS FOR THAT!

OK... SO, HOW MUCH FURTHER TO YOUR HEALING MINIMARKET, THEN?

BEHIND THE NEXT BLOCK THERE...

THAT BUILDING! THAT'S THE ONE!

!!!

SAM?! DID YOU SENSE SOMETHING?!

QUICK! FOLLOW ME! WE CAN'T STAY HERE!

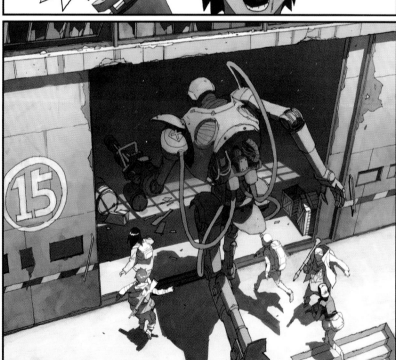

36

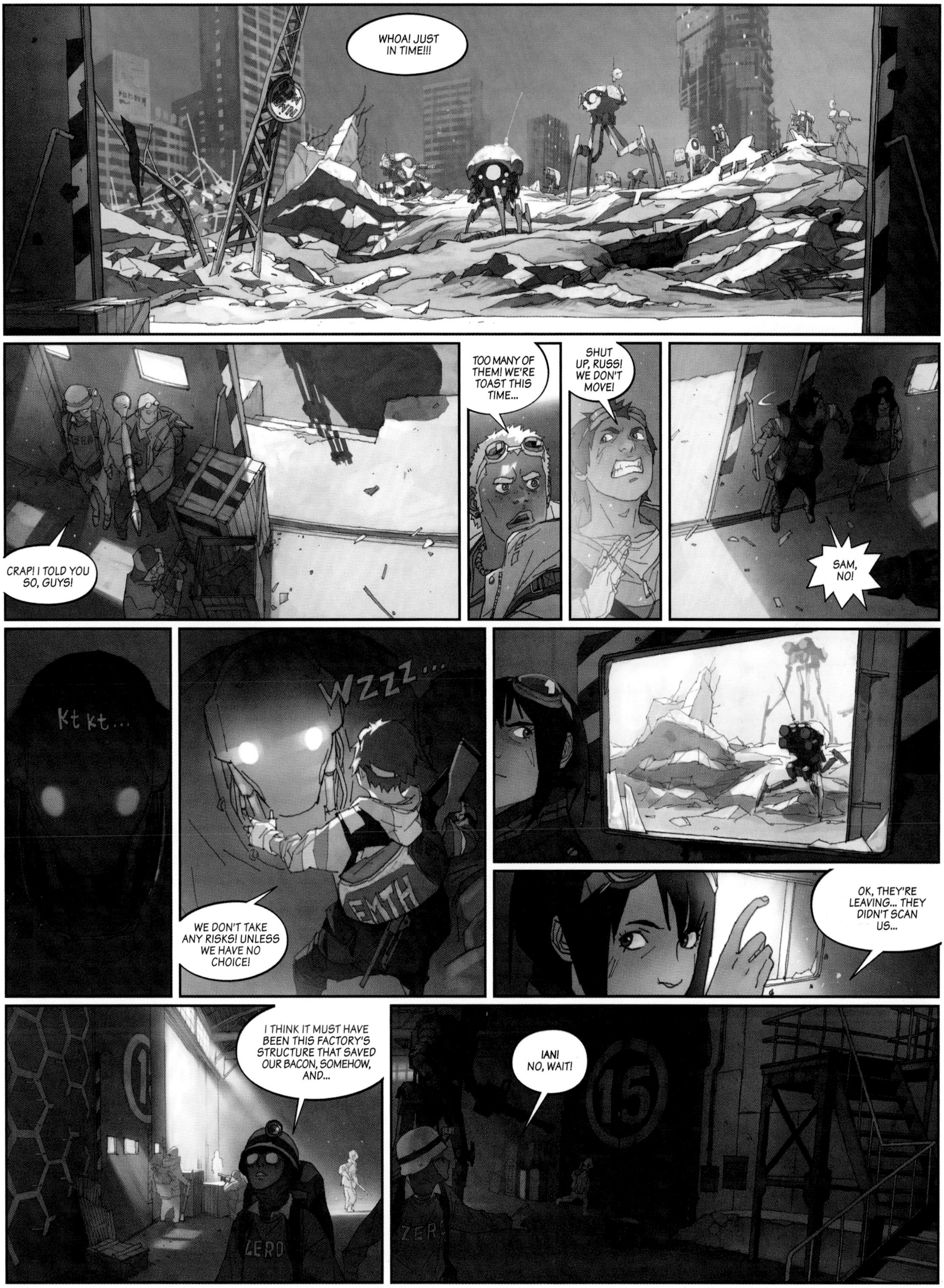
WHOA! JUST IN TIME!!!
CRAP! I TOLD YOU SO, GUYS!
TOO MANY OF THEM! WE'RE TOAST THIS TIME...
SHUT UP, RUSS! WE DON'T MOVE!
SAM, NO!
Kt kt...
WZZZ...
WE DON'T TAKE ANY RISKS! UNLESS WE HAVE NO CHOICE!
OK, THEY'RE LEAVING... THEY DIDN'T SCAN US...
I THINK IT MUST HAVE BEEN THIS FACTORY'S STRUCTURE THAT SAVED OUR BACON, SOMEHOW, AND...
IAN! NO, WAIT!

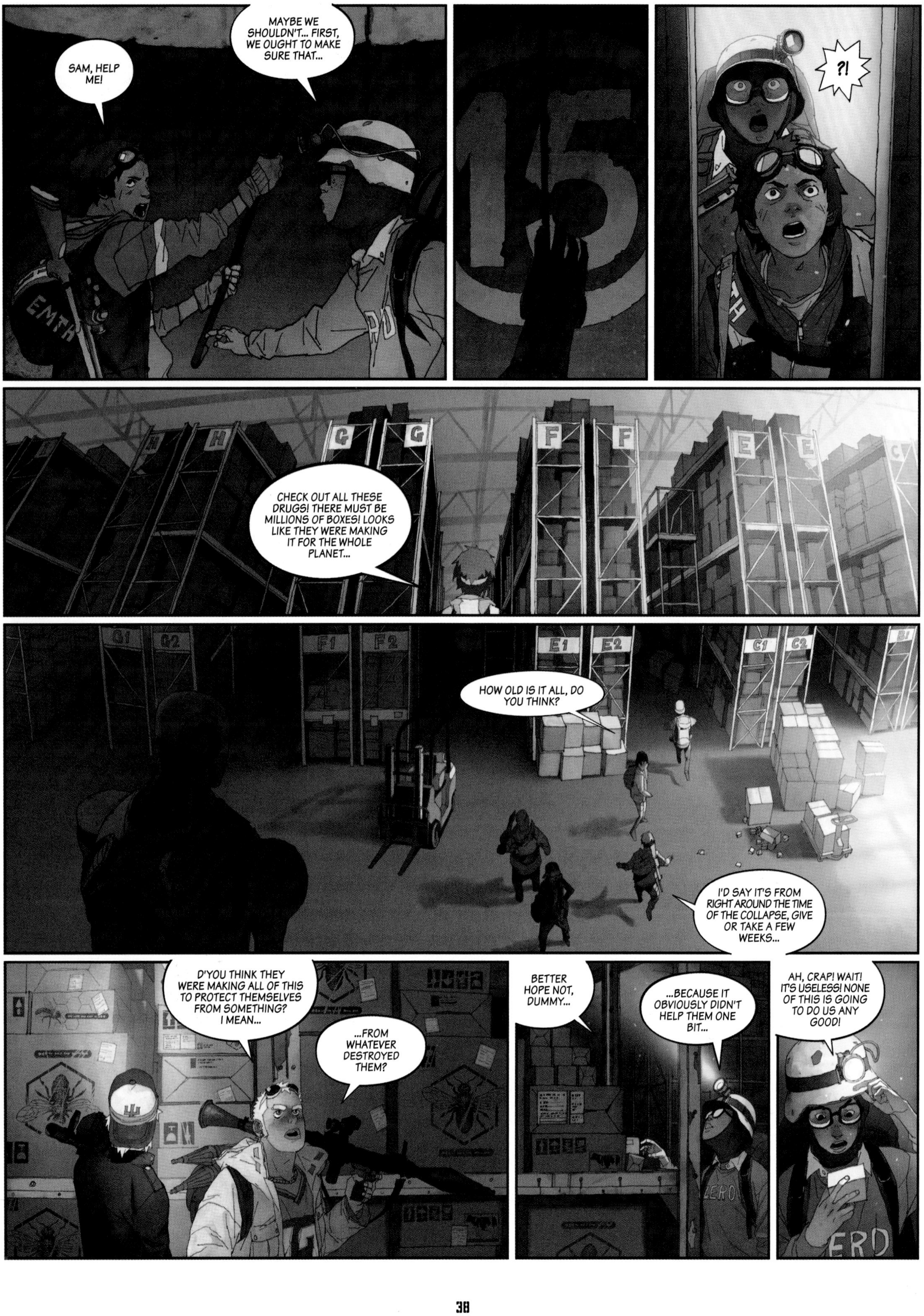
SAM, HELP ME!
MAYBE WE SHOULDN'T... FIRST, WE OUGHT TO MAKE SURE THAT...
15
?!
G
G
F
F
E
E
CHECK OUT ALL THESE DRUGS! THERE MUST BE MILLIONS OF BOXES! LOOKS LIKE THEY WERE MAKING IT FOR THE WHOLE PLANET...
G1
G2
F1
F2
E1
E2
C1
C2
HOW OLD IS IT ALL, DO YOU THINK?
I'D SAY IT'S FROM RIGHT AROUND THE TIME OF THE COLLAPSE, GIVE OR TAKE A FEW WEEKS...
D'YOU THINK THEY WERE MAKING ALL OF THIS TO PROTECT THEMSELVES FROM SOMETHING? I MEAN...
...FROM WHATEVER DESTROYED THEM?
BETTER HOPE NOT, DUMMY...
...BECAUSE IT OBVIOUSLY DIDN'T HELP THEM ONE BIT...
AH, CRAP! WAIT! IT'S USELESS! NONE OF THIS IS GOING TO DO US ANY GOOD!

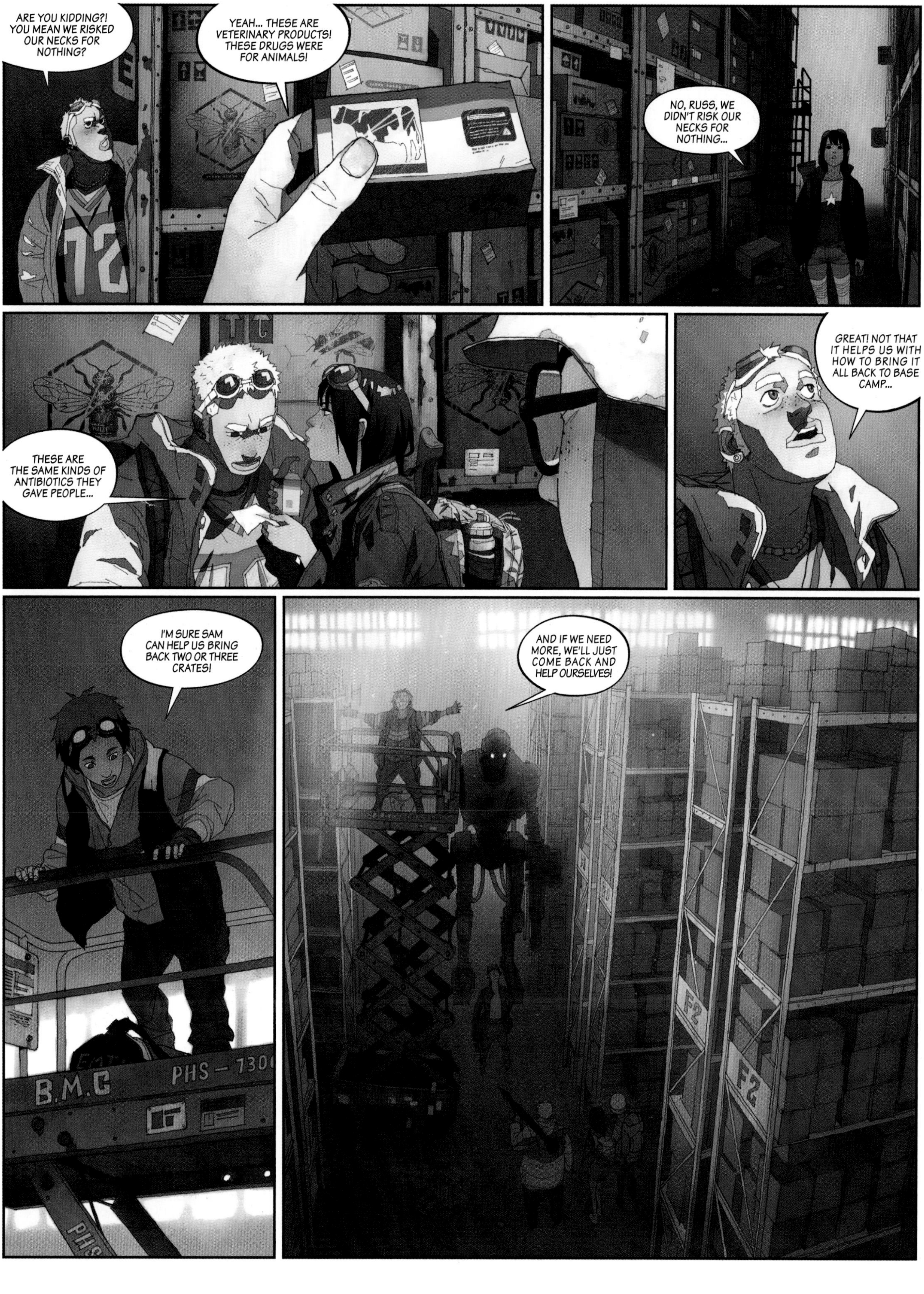
ARE YOU KIDDING?! YOU MEAN WE RISKED OUR NECKS FOR NOTHING?
YEAH... THESE ARE VETERINARY PRODUCTS! THESE DRUGS WERE FOR ANIMALS!
NO, RUSS, WE DIDN'T RISK OUR NECKS FOR NOTHING...
THESE ARE THE SAME KINDS OF ANTIBIOTICS THEY GAVE PEOPLE...
GREAT! NOT THAT IT HELPS US WITH HOW TO BRING IT ALL BACK TO BASE CAMP...
I'M SURE SAM CAN HELP US BRING BACK TWO OR THREE CRATES!
B.M.C PHS-730
AND IF WE NEED MORE, WE'LL JUST COME BACK AND HELP OURSELVES!
F2
F2

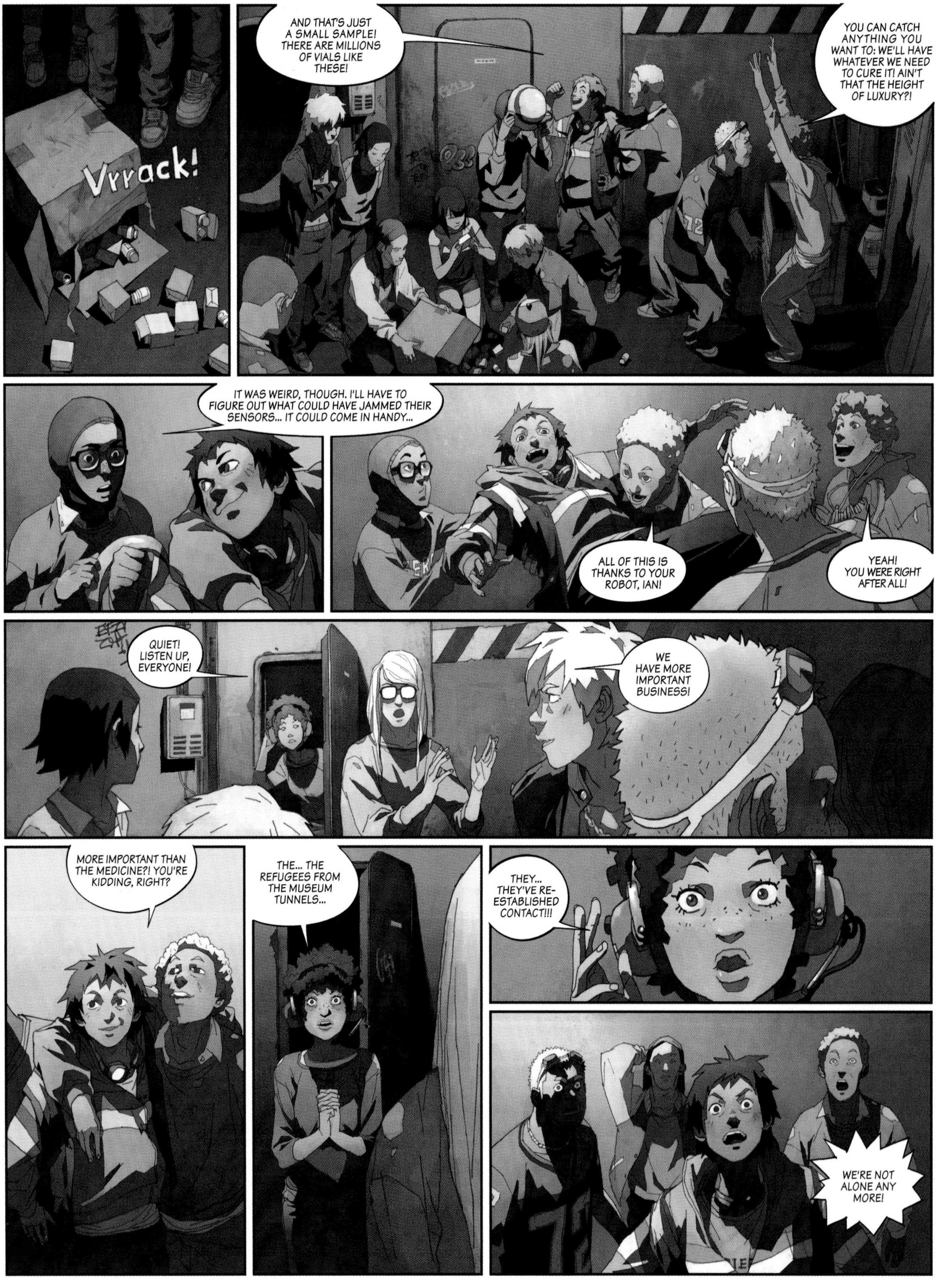
Vrrack!
AND THAT'S JUST A SMALL SAMPLE! THERE ARE MILLIONS OF VIALS LIKE THESE!
YOU CAN CATCH ANYTHING YOU WANT TO: WE'LL HAVE WHATEVER WE NEED TO CURE IT! AIN'T THAT THE HEIGHT OF LUXURY?!
IT WAS WEIRD, THOUGH. I'LL HAVE TO FIGURE OUT WHAT COULD HAVE JAMMED THEIR SENSORS... IT COULD COME IN HANDY...
ALL OF THIS IS THANKS TO YOUR ROBOT, IAN!
YEAH! YOU WERE RIGHT AFTER ALL!
QUIET! LISTEN UP, EVERYONE!
WE HAVE MORE IMPORTANT BUSINESS!
MORE IMPORTANT THAN THE MEDICINE?! YOU'RE KIDDING, RIGHT?
THE... THE REFUGEES FROM THE MUSEUM TUNNELS...
THEY... THEY'VE RE-ESTABLISHED CONTACT!!!
WE'RE NOT ALONE ANY MORE!

THE PICTURE ISN'T CLEAR AND THE SOUND'S A LITTLE TINNY, BUT IT'S STILL INTELLIGIBLE...

I'M PRETTY SURE I RECOGNISED PHIL, THEIR LEADER...

HE LOOKS TIRED — HE MAY EVEN BE SICK — BUT IT'S HIM...

WE'VE WAITED FOR YOU FOR SO LONG... WHY DID YOU BREAK OFF CONTACT?

AFTER THE ATTACK ON OUR MUSEUM HIDEOUT, WE WERE FORCED TO HIDE SOMEWHERE ELSE...

WE'RE OUT OF DRUGS, BUT WE STILL HAVE FOOD. MAYBE WE COULD TRADE...

THAT'S ALL I COULD RECORD BEFORE WE WERE CUT OFF...

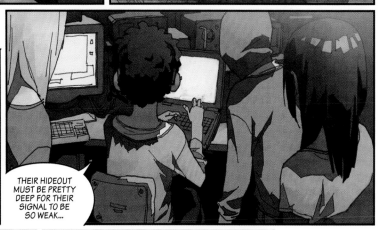

THEIR HIDEOUT MUST BE PRETTY DEEP FOR THEIR SIGNAL TO BE SO WEAK...

...BUT I NARROWED THEIR LOCATION TO THIS AREA...

GREAT! TOMORROW, WE'LL SEND THEM SOME EMISSARIES...

IAN, AFTER WHAT YOU ACCOMPLISHED TODAY...

...YOU AND YOUR TEAM ARE THE OBVIOUS CHOICE FOR RE-ESTABLISHING CONTACT...

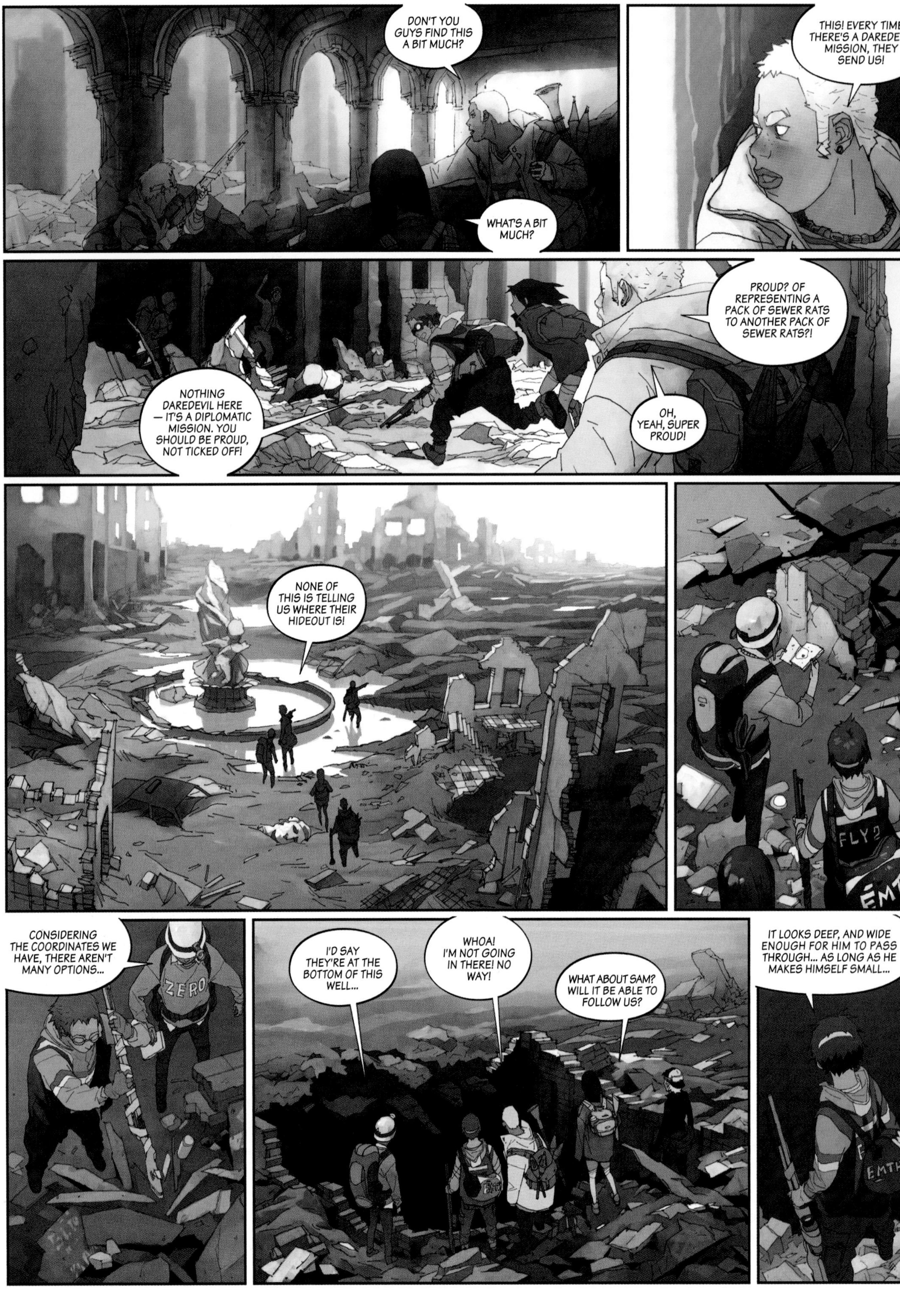
DON'T YOU GUYS FIND THIS A BIT MUCH?
WHAT'S A BIT MUCH?
THIS! EVERY TIME THERE'S A DAREDEVIL MISSION, THEY SEND US!
NOTHING DAREDEVIL HERE — IT'S A DIPLOMATIC MISSION. YOU SHOULD BE PROUD, NOT TICKED OFF!
PROUD? OF REPRESENTING A PACK OF SEWER RATS TO ANOTHER PACK OF SEWER RATS?!
OH, YEAH, SUPER PROUD!
NONE OF THIS IS TELLING US WHERE THEIR HIDEOUT IS!
FLY2
EMTH
CONSIDERING THE COORDINATES WE HAVE, THERE AREN'T MANY OPTIONS...
ZERO
I'D SAY THEY'RE AT THE BOTTOM OF THIS WELL...
WHOA! I'M NOT GOING IN THERE! NO WAY!
WHAT ABOUT SAM? WILL IT BE ABLE TO FOLLOW US?
IT LOOKS DEEP, AND WIDE ENOUGH FOR HIM TO PASS THROUGH... AS LONG AS HE MAKES HIMSELF SMALL...
EMTH

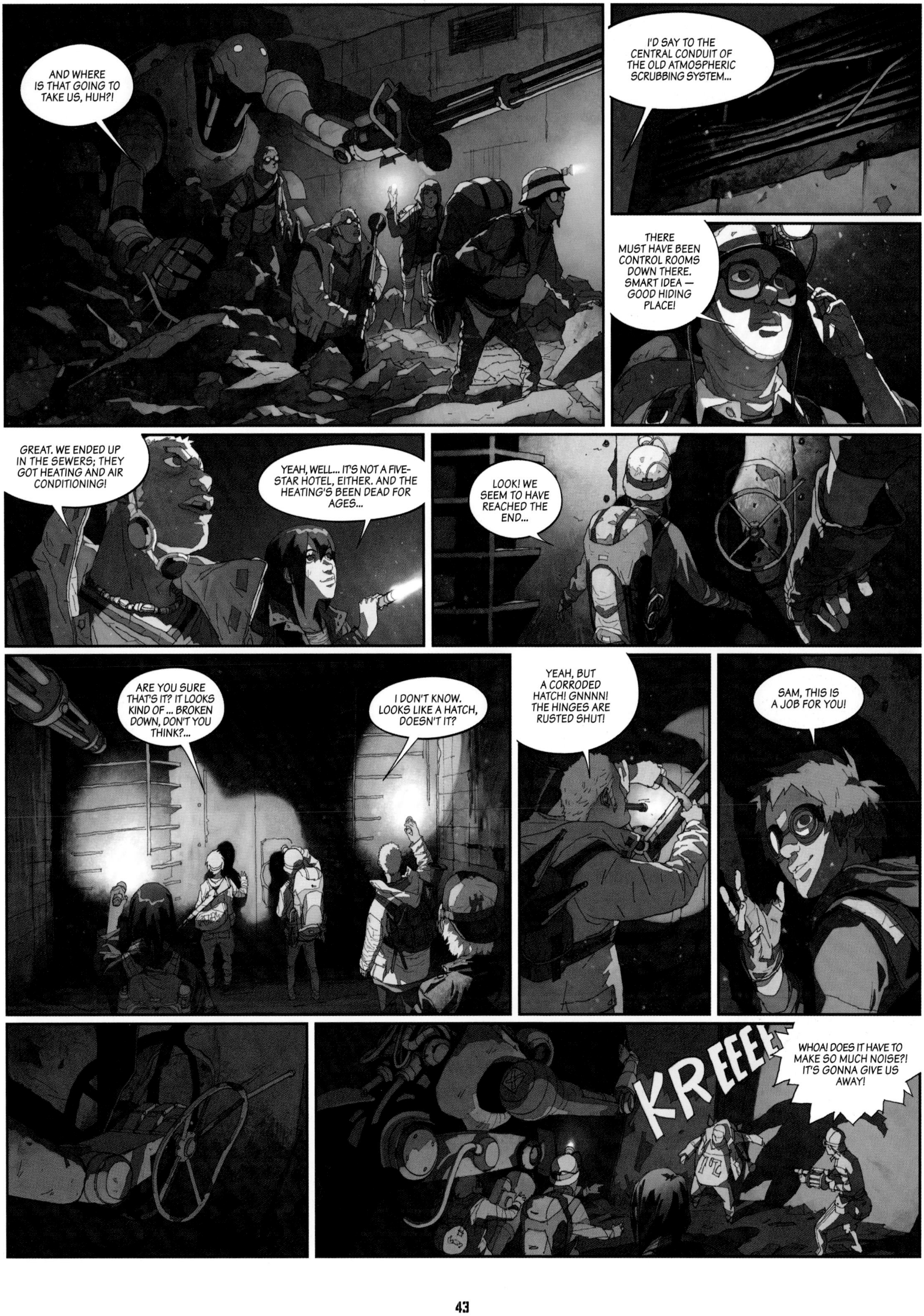
AND WHERE IS THAT GOING TO TAKE US, HUH?!
I'D SAY TO THE CENTRAL CONDUIT OF THE OLD ATMOSPHERIC SCRUBBING SYSTEM...
THERE MUST HAVE BEEN CONTROL ROOMS DOWN THERE. SMART IDEA — GOOD HIDING PLACE!
GREAT. WE ENDED UP IN THE SEWERS; THEY GOT HEATING AND AIR CONDITIONING!
YEAH, WELL... IT'S NOT A FIVE-STAR HOTEL, EITHER. AND THE HEATING'S BEEN DEAD FOR AGES...
LOOK! WE SEEM TO HAVE REACHED THE END...
ARE YOU SURE THAT'S IT? IT LOOKS KIND OF ... BROKEN DOWN, DON'T YOU THINK?...
I DON'T KNOW. LOOKS LIKE A HATCH, DOESN'T IT?
YEAH, BUT A CORRODED HATCH! GNNNN! THE HINGES ARE RUSTED SHUT!
SAM, THIS IS A JOB FOR YOU!
KREEEE
WHOA! DOES IT HAVE TO MAKE SO MUCH NOISE?! IT'S GONNA GIVE US AWAY!

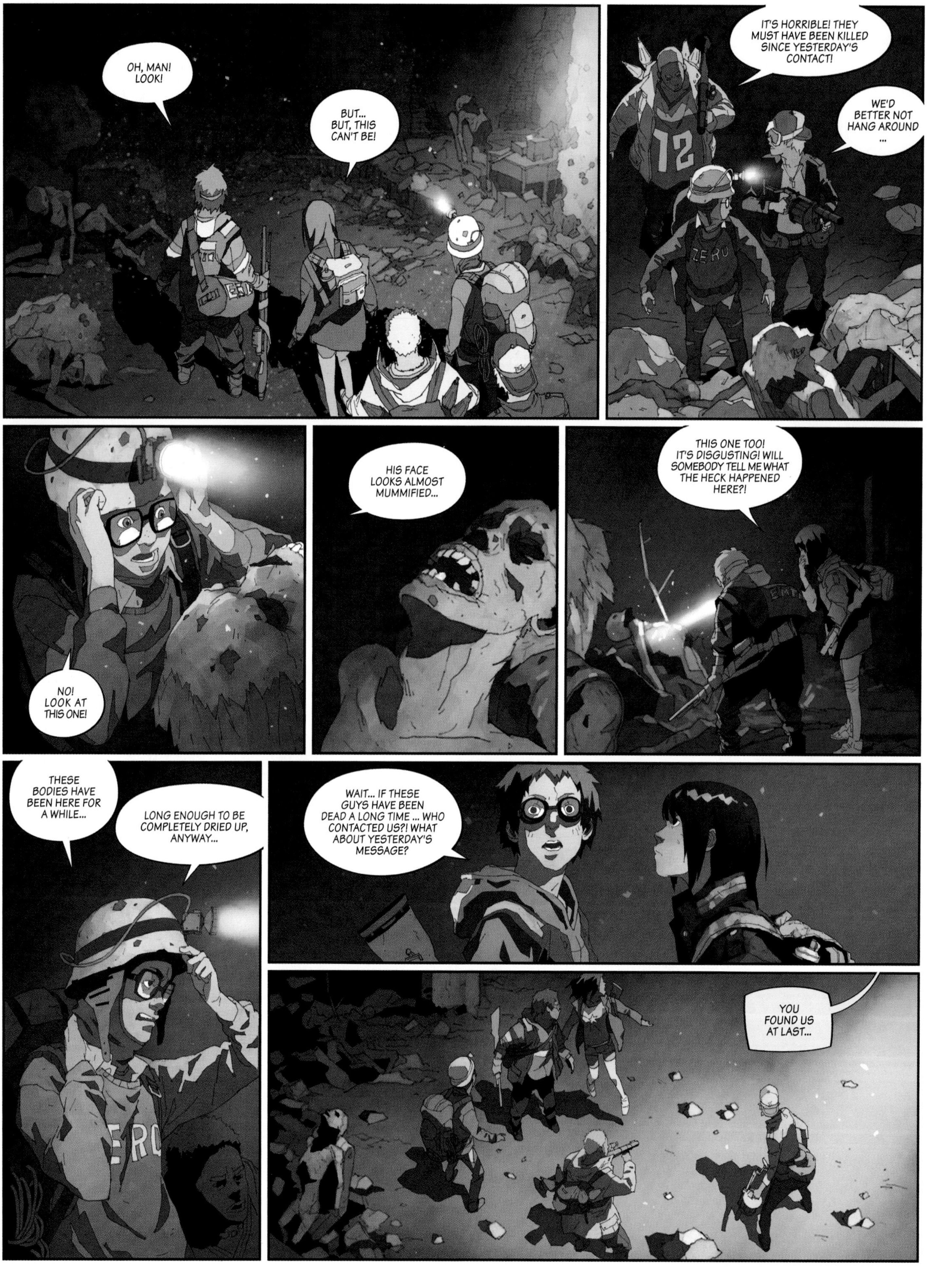
OH, MAN! LOOK!
BUT... BUT, THIS CAN'T BE!
IT'S HORRIBLE! THEY MUST HAVE BEEN KILLED SINCE YESTERDAY'S CONTACT!
WE'D BETTER NOT HANG AROUND ...
NO! LOOK AT THIS ONE!
HIS FACE LOOKS ALMOST MUMMIFIED...
THIS ONE TOO! IT'S DISGUSTING! WILL SOMEBODY TELL ME WHAT THE HECK HAPPENED HERE?!
THESE BODIES HAVE BEEN HERE FOR A WHILE...
LONG ENOUGH TO BE COMPLETELY DRIED UP, ANYWAY...
WAIT... IF THESE GUYS HAVE BEEN DEAD A LONG TIME ... WHO CONTACTED US?! WHAT ABOUT YESTERDAY'S MESSAGE?
YOU FOUND US AT LAST...

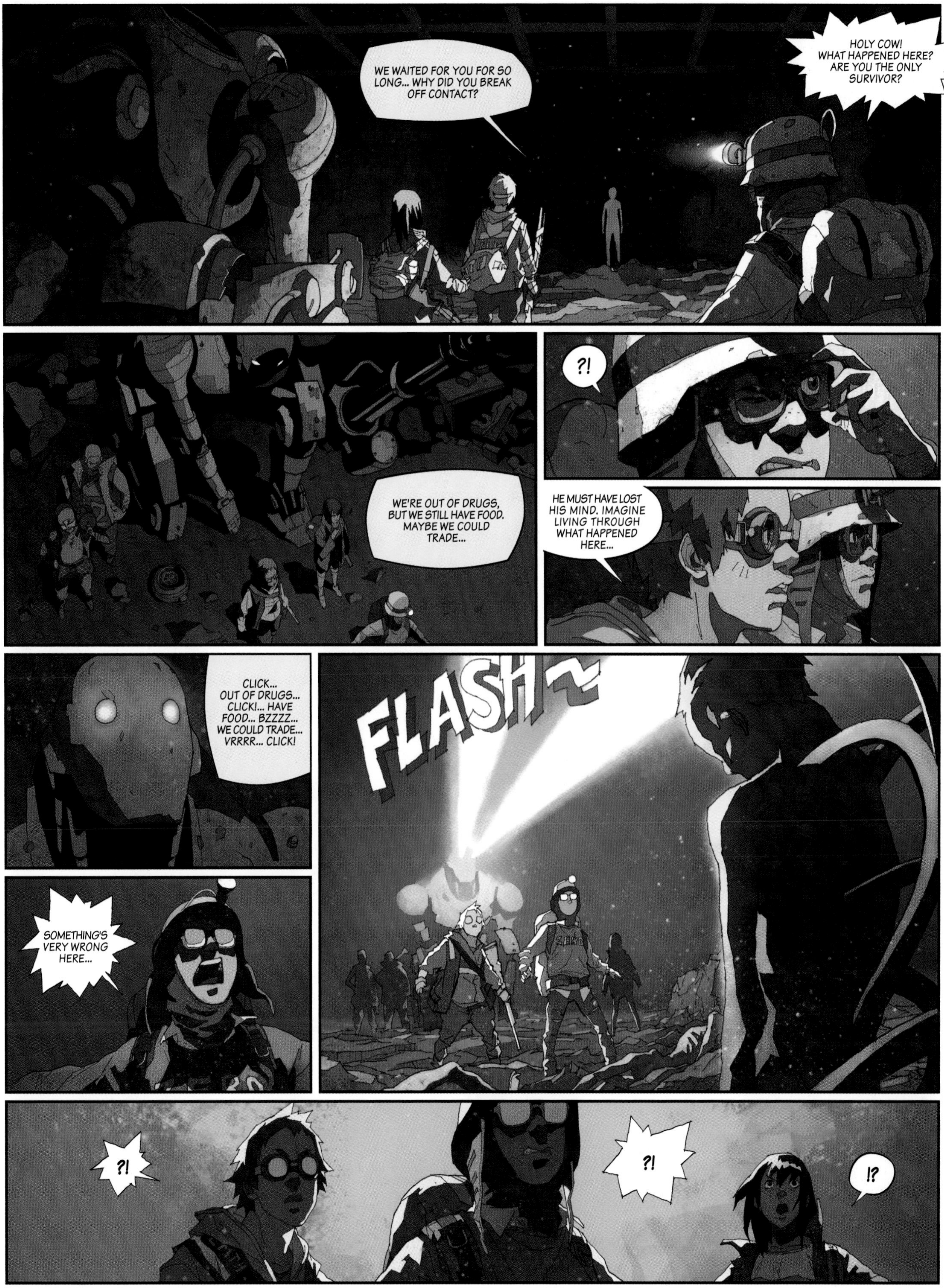
WE WAITED FOR YOU FOR SO LONG... WHY DID YOU BREAK OFF CONTACT?
HOLY COW! WHAT HAPPENED HERE? ARE YOU THE ONLY SURVIVOR?
WE'RE OUT OF DRUGS, BUT WE STILL HAVE FOOD. MAYBE WE COULD TRADE...
?!
HE MUST HAVE LOST HIS MIND. IMAGINE LIVING THROUGH WHAT HAPPENED HERE...
CLICK... OUT OF DRUGS... CLICK!... HAVE FOOD... BZZZZ... WE COULD TRADE... VRRRR... CLICK!
SOMETHING'S VERY WRONG HERE...
FLASH
?!
?!
!?

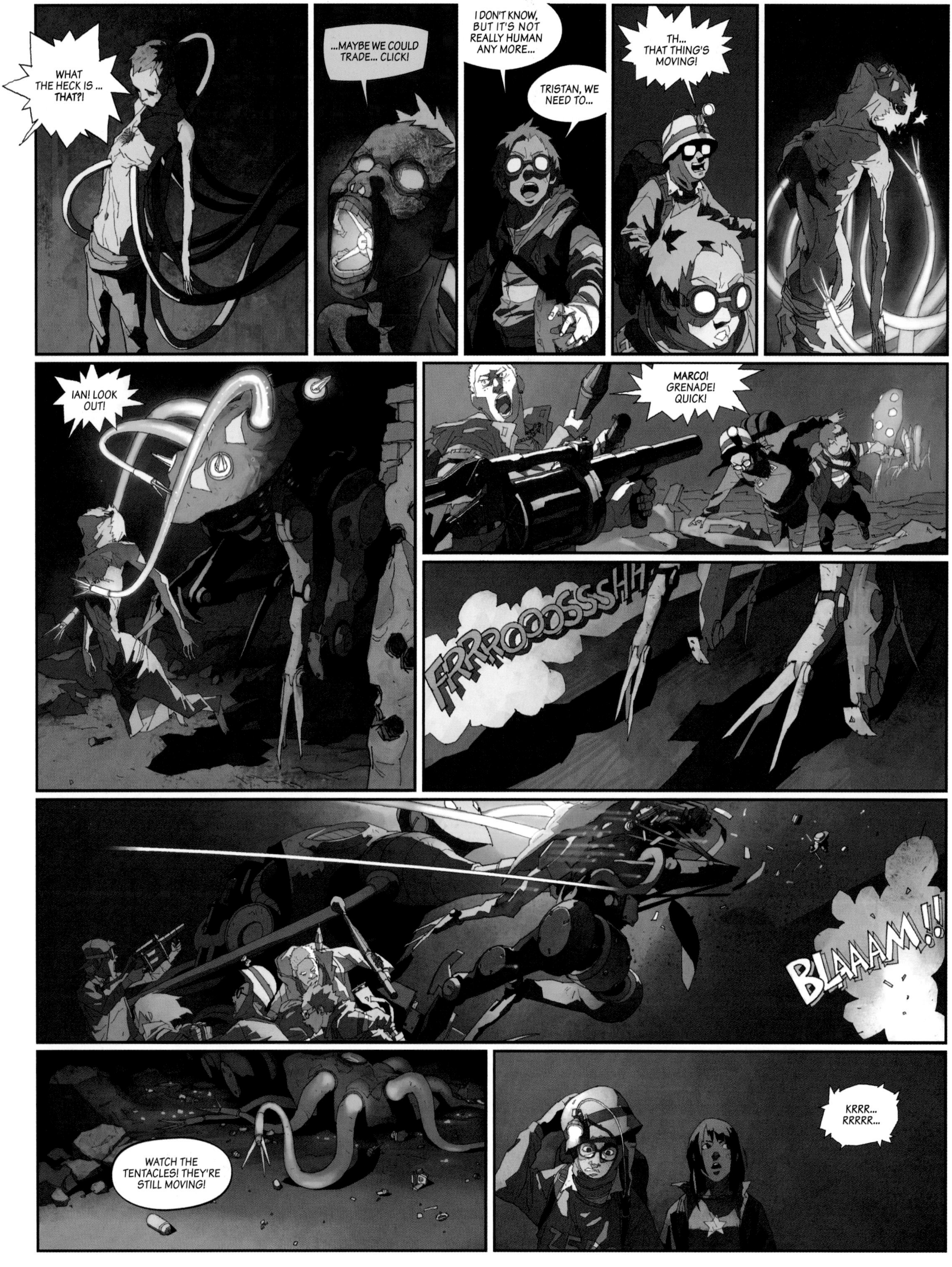
WHAT THE HECK IS ... THAT?!
...MAYBE WE COULD TRADE... CLICK!
I DON'T KNOW, BUT IT'S NOT REALLY HUMAN ANY MORE...
TRISTAN, WE NEED TO...
TH... THAT THING'S MOVING!
IAN! LOOK OUT!
MARCO! GRENADE! QUICK!
FRRROOOSSSHH!
BLAAAM!!
WATCH THE TENTACLES! THEY'RE STILL MOVING!
KRRR... RRRRR...

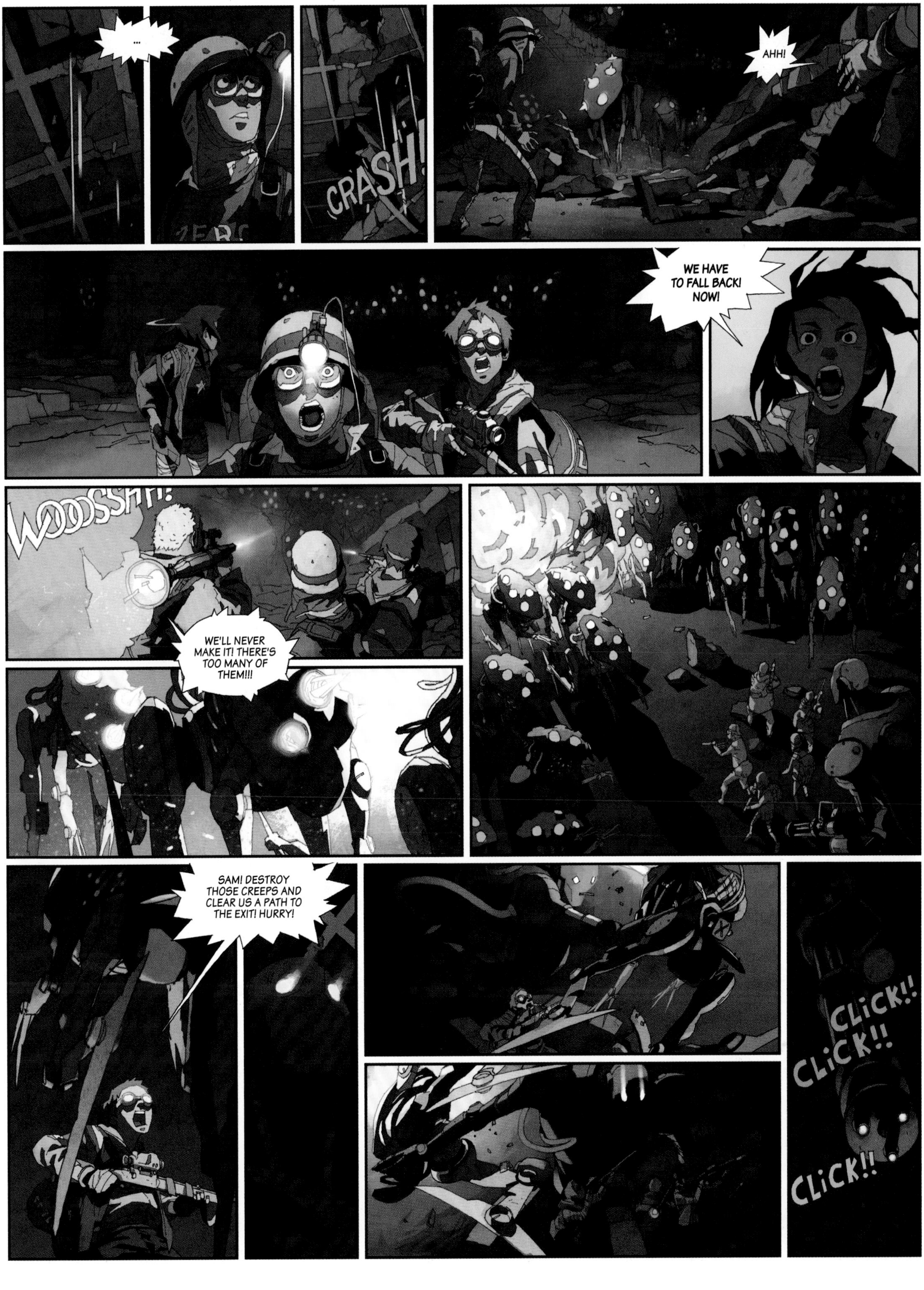
...
CRASH!
AHH!
WE HAVE TO FALL BACK! NOW!
WOOOSSHH!
WE'LL NEVER MAKE IT! THERE'S TOO MANY OF THEM!!!
SAM! DESTROY THOSE CREEPS AND CLEAR US A PATH TO THE EXIT! HURRY!
CLICK!!
CLICK!!
CLICK!!

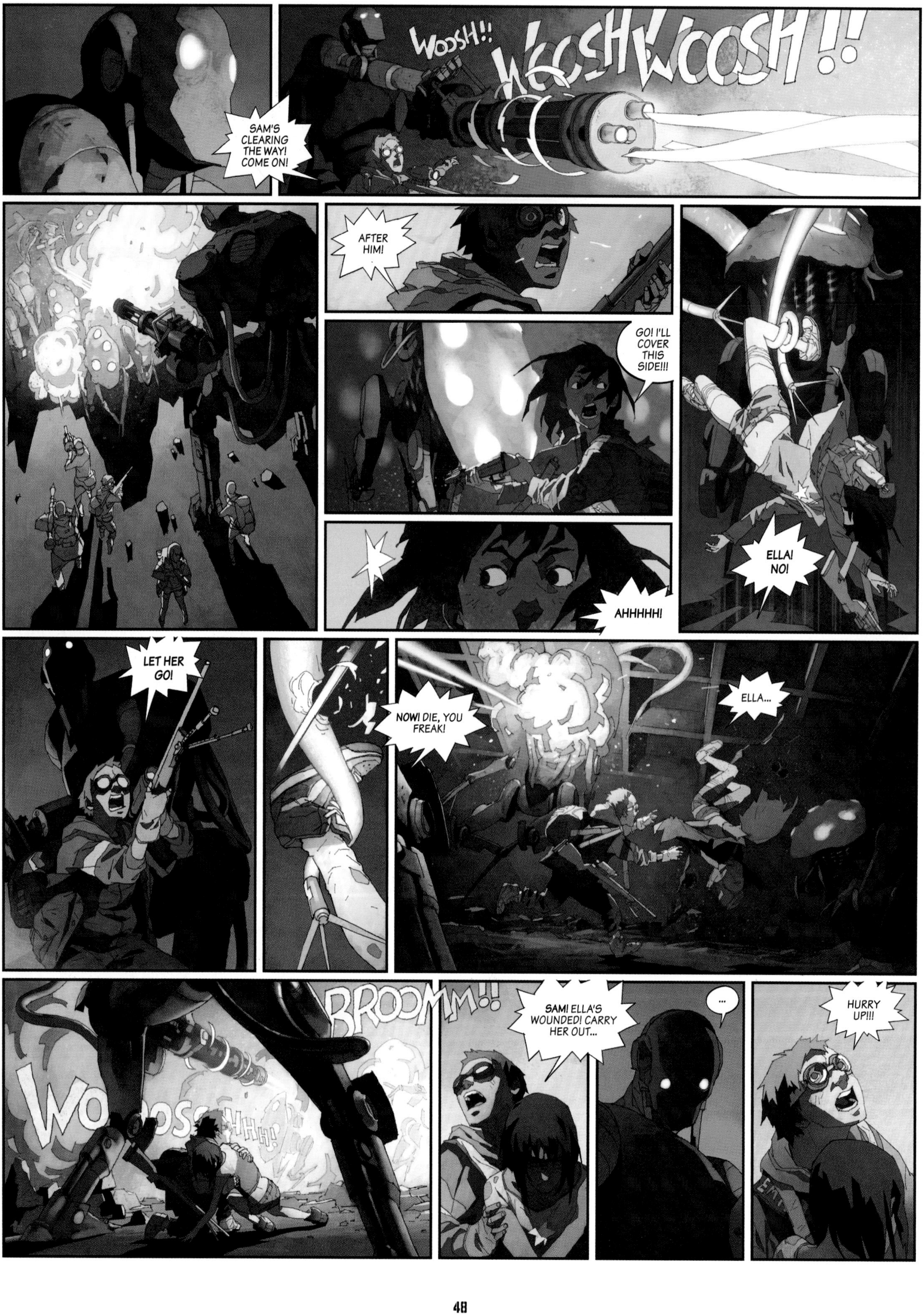
SAM'S CLEARING THE WAY! COME ON!
WOOSH!!
WOOSHWOOSH!!
AFTER HIM!
GO! I'LL COVER THIS SIDE!!!
AHHHHH!
ELLA! NO!
LET HER GO!
NOW! DIE, YOU FREAK!
ELLA...
BROOMM!!
SAM! ELLA'S WOUNDED! CARRY HER OUT...
...
HURRY UP!!!

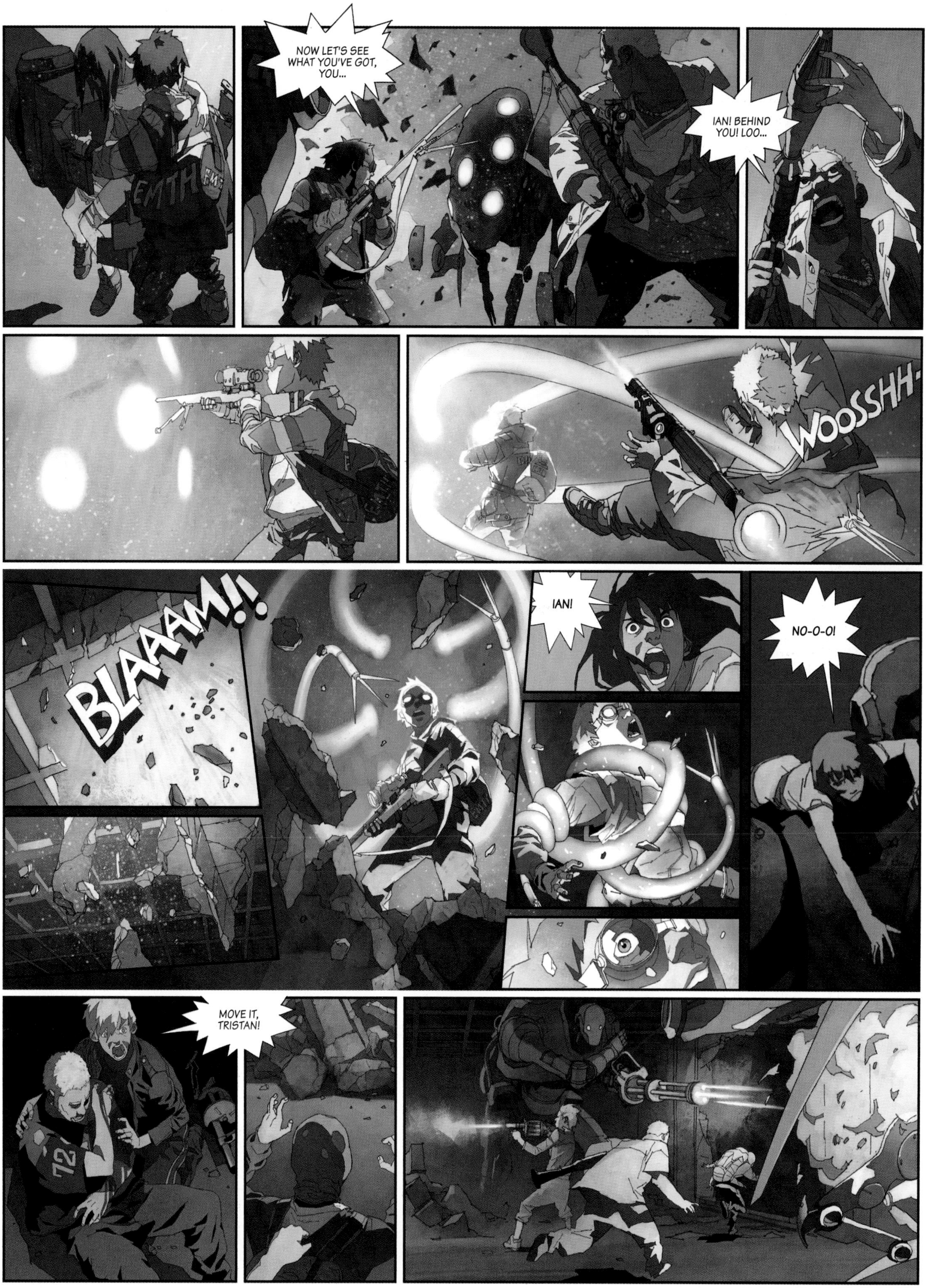
NOW LET'S SEE WHAT YOU'VE GOT, YOU...
IAN! BEHIND YOU! LOO...
WOOSSHH
BLAAAM!!
IAN!
NO-O-O!
MOVE IT, TRISTAN!

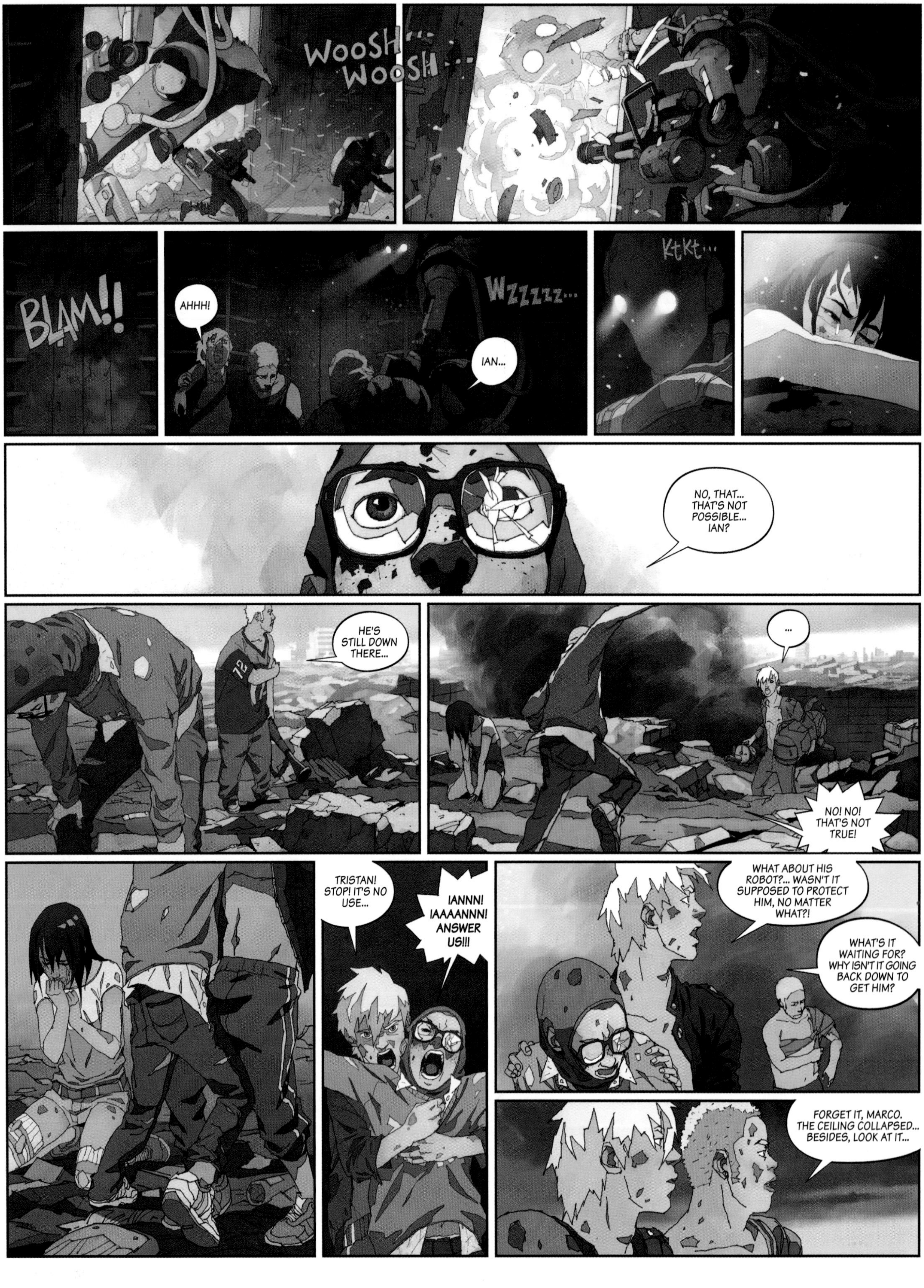
WOOSH...
WOOSH...
BLAM!!
AHHH!
IAN...
WZZZZZ...
KTKT...
NO, THAT... THAT'S NOT POSSIBLE... IAN?
HE'S STILL DOWN THERE...
...
NO! NO! THAT'S NOT TRUE!
TRISTAN! STOP! IT'S NO USE...
IANNN! IAAAANNN! ANSWER US!!!
WHAT ABOUT HIS ROBOT?... WASN'T IT SUPPOSED TO PROTECT HIM, NO MATTER WHAT?!
WHAT'S IT WAITING FOR? WHY ISN'T IT GOING BACK DOWN TO GET HIM?
FORGET IT, MARCO. THE CEILING COLLAPSED... BESIDES, LOOK AT IT...

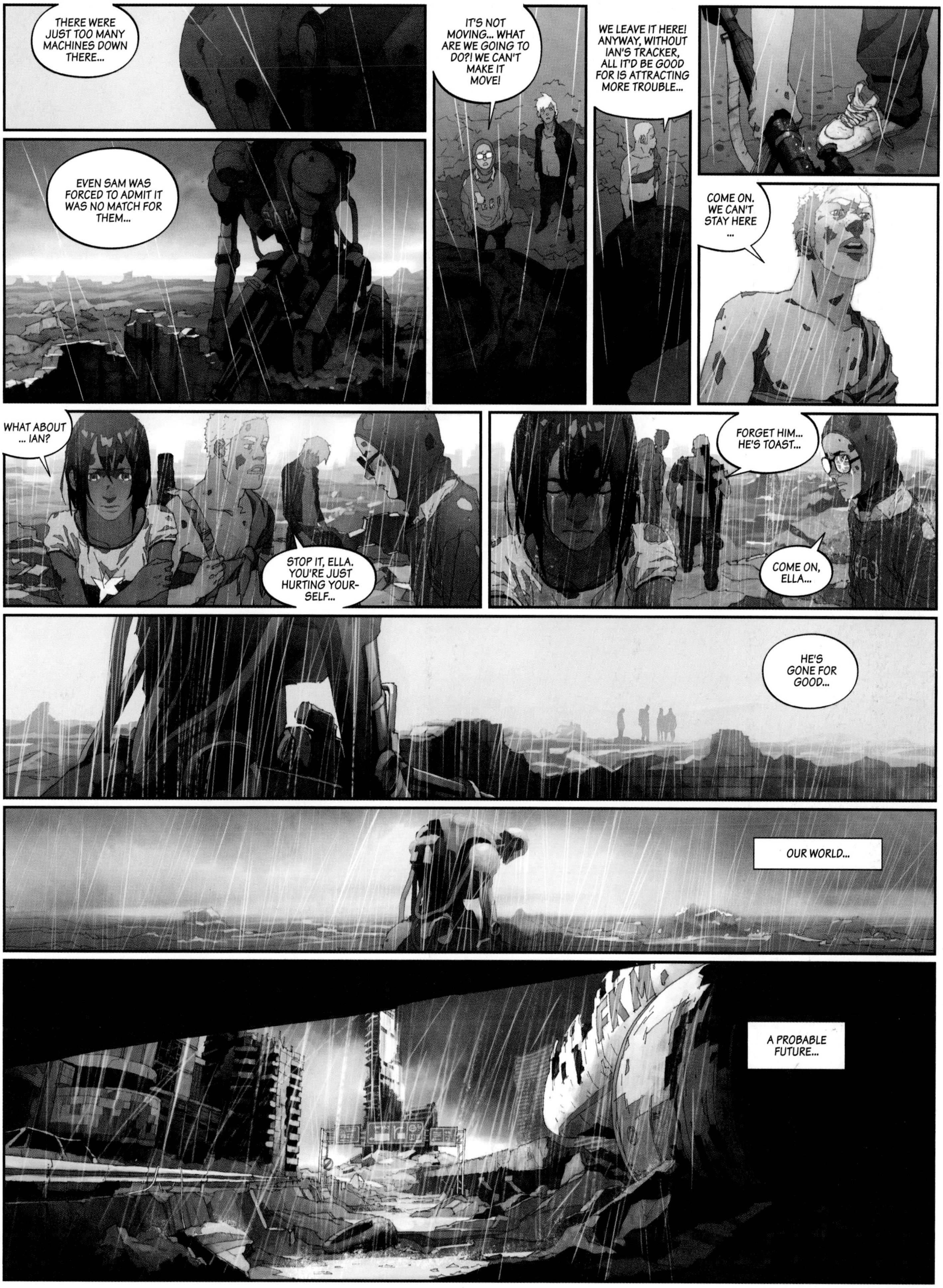
THERE WERE JUST TOO MANY MACHINES DOWN THERE...
IT'S NOT MOVING... WHAT ARE WE GOING TO DO?! WE CAN'T MAKE IT MOVE!
WE LEAVE IT HERE! ANYWAY, WITHOUT IAN'S TRACKER, ALL IT'D BE GOOD FOR IS ATTRACTING MORE TROUBLE...
EVEN SAM WAS FORCED TO ADMIT IT WAS NO MATCH FOR THEM...
COME ON. WE CAN'T STAY HERE ...
WHAT ABOUT ... IAN?
STOP IT, ELLA. YOU'RE JUST HURTING YOURSELF...
FORGET HIM... HE'S TOAST...
COME ON, ELLA...
HE'S GONE FOR GOOD...
OUR WORLD...
A PROBABLE FUTURE...

TO BE CONTINUED...

COMING SOON

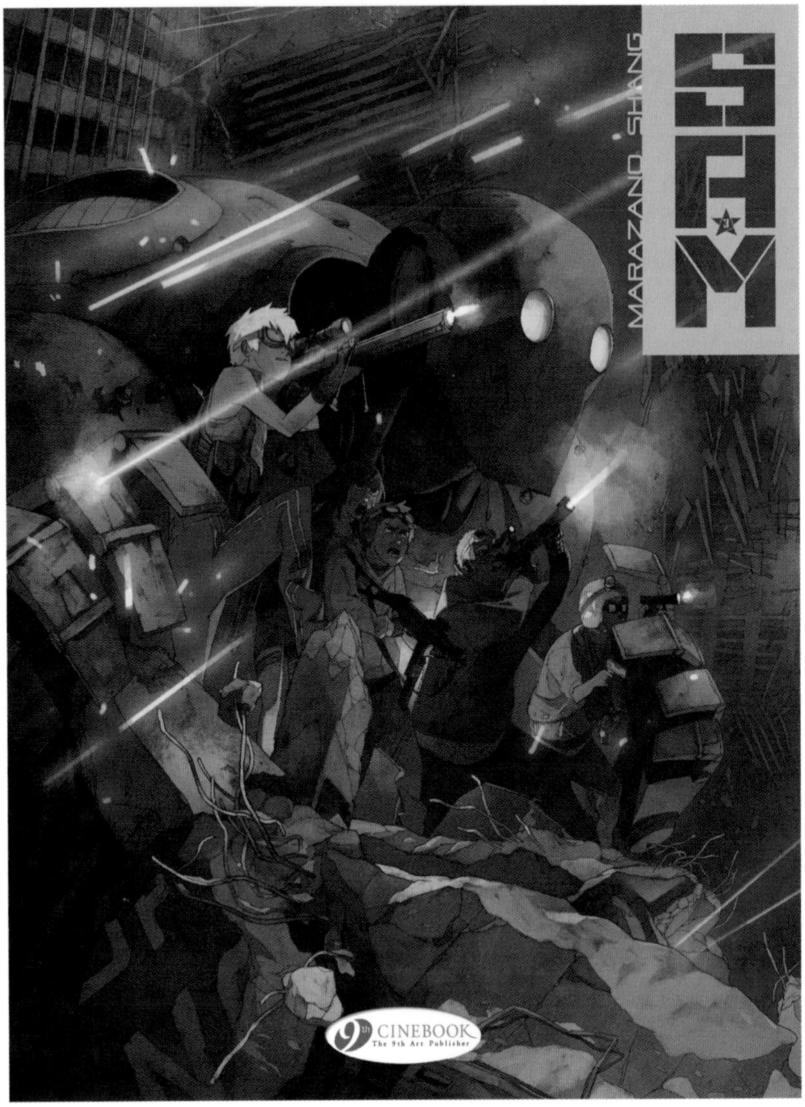
MARAZANO SHANG
S.A.M
CINEBOOK
The 9th Art Publisher

A MILLION WINTERS